PROVEN WORD books have proven
themselves where it counts — among the
thousands of readers who have made them
best-sellers because they found them
meaningful in the arena of life.

These books were best-sellers in hardcover
and are now offered at a more affordable
price in deluxe paperback bindings.

These special editions also offer you a
built-in study guide with insightful questions
which will encourage group discussions as
well as personal reflection and thought.

The *Proven Word* series addresses the
widespread needs of people everywhere
who are searching for the answers to the
pressures and problems of living in
today's modern world.

PRAYER
KEY TO REVIVAL

PRAYER
KEY TO REVIVAL
PAUL Y. CHO

WORD PUBLISHING
Dallas · London · Sydney · Singapore

Library of Congress Cataloging in Publication Data

Cho, Yong-gi, 1936–
  Prayer, the key to revival.

  1. Prayer.   2. Church renewal.   I. Manzano,
R. Whitney. II. Title.
BV215.C54   1984   248.3′2   84-15255
ISBN 0–8499–3073–1 (paperback)

  9801239 RRD 987

Printed in the United States of America

If my people, which are called by my name,
shall humble themselves, and pray, and seek my face,
and turn from their wicked ways; then will I hear
from heaven, and will forgive their sin, and will
heal their land

2 CHRONICLES 7:14

Contents

PART III. The Forms of Prayer

PART IV: Methods of Prayer

PART V: The Powerful Prayer Is Based on the Blood
    Covenant in Christ Jesus

Introduction

△

As I write this book, my church is growing at the rate of twelve thousand new converts every month. These new souls are being saved from Buddhism, secularism and nominal Christian backgrounds. No one can argue that this unprecedented rate of church growth is due to the revival fires now sweeping over Korea.

The present membership of our church is approaching 400,000. By the end of 1984, at our present rate of growth, we shall have in excess of 500,000 active members.

How could a church grow this large?

Is it possible for other countries to have this kind of revival?

I am convinced that renewal is possible anywhere people dedicate themselves to prayer.

It is because I believe in revival and renewal that I have written this book. It has been historically true that prayer has been the key to every revival in the history of Christianity.

Before the church was born on the Day of Pentecost, Luke wrote "and (the disciples) were continually in the temple, praising and blessing God" (Luke 24:53). Luke further amplifies what the disciples were doing: "These all continued with one accord in prayer and supplication . . ." (Acts 1:14). Therefore the church was born when the Holy Spirit descended during a time of concentrated prayer.

Before the missionary era of the church began, the Holy Spirit revealed to the leaders gathered in Antioch that they should send Barnabas and Saul. Yet, the Holy Spirit only spoke after they had been in fasting and prayer.

Martin Luther was not satisfied with the religious world in which he was born. His deep need for personal piety caused him to spend much time in prayer while he was Professor of Theology at the University of Wittenberg. During the winter of 1512, he locked himself in a room within the tower of the Black Monastery at Wittenburg and prayed over what he was discovering in the Scriptures. The Reformation was born after that season of prayer and study. The Reformation gave us the biblical truth of Justification by Faith. Man no longer could work for his salvation, but salvation was the gift of God through faith.

After the fires of revival that spread throughout Europe began to wane, the Enlightenment arose. As this new movement began in the arts and spread to every sector of European society, there was a revival of the pagan concept of man's supreme worth. Reason became the means by which truth and reality would be judged and faith appeared unimportant. What was needed was a fresh movement of the Holy Spirit.

John Wesley, the son of an Anglican clergyman from Epworth, England, was dissatisfied with the state of the Church of England. He was deeply moved by the great need of the poor who had flocked to the cities where they lived in deplorable conditions. On the evening of 24 May 1738, at a quarter of nine, as he was listening to the reading of Luther's preface to the Epistle to the Romans, John Wesley experienced a genuine conversion. He was born again. This led to much prayer and fasting for John, Charles, his brother, and George Whitfield. As the Church of England closed its doors to their ministry, they began ministering to large crowds not only in Great Britain, but also in America. Thousands gathered to hear the freshly anointed preaching of the Word of God. As a result, the world-wide Methodist revival was born.

In the nineteenth century the Protestant church again veered from the course set by the early Reformers and sank into what was called "higher criticism." The result was that people started leaving the traditional churches, not for other groups, but they simply stayed home. Toward the end of the century, God raised up evangelists like Charles Finney, Dwight L. Moody and R. A. Torrey. These men preached under the anointing of the Holy Spirit, motivated by continual prayer and fasting.

The spiritual climate was rising again as the twentieth century rolled in. In 1905 in Los Angeles, California, the Holy Spirit fell again. Methodists and Holiness Christians had been fasting and praying for revival when the Holy Spirit fell as in the second chapter of the Book of Acts. The Holy Spirit had given those who were assembled together the gift of tongues. This revival, which was later called Pentecostalism, has spread throughout the world.

Now, we are in the latter part of the twentieth century. Many Pentecostals and Charismatics (members or former members of traditional churches who exercise the gift of tongues) are feeling the same secularism that has crept into much of the church. What is needed in the church today is a new outpouring of the Holy Spirit. What will bring about the revival that can lead the world away from the brink of total destruction and annihilation? The answer is a new call to prayer!

At no time in the history of the modern world has there been such an outpouring of Satanic influence as there is today. The bottom of the pit of hell is belching out its filth in murder, rape, pornography, lawlessness and so on. Just as the preaching of the Wesleys kept Britain from following France in revolution in the eighteenth century, so too a new outbreak of revival can bring about the social and political changes necessary to keep us from international destruction and calamity.

Therefore, this book has importance for you and for those whom you will affect. Since you have started reading this book, I assume you are interested in prayer.

I am convinced that the reason the Holy Spirit has brought you to this book is this: you already know you need to pray. My desire is to share with you from my personal life and ministry so that you will be motivated to pray.

I also want you to know *why* you should pray, *how* you should pray and *when* you should pray. In order for you to know this, you must understand the many different kinds of prayer that exist.

What is the link between prayer and fasting? Why does fasting increase the effectiveness of prayer? Is it important to pray in an unknown language? These and many other questions are addressed in this book.

I sincerely believe that after reading this book you will never be the same. Your prayers will have more power! There will be a marked change in your life! Your ministry will be more effective!

I am working on one simple premise. That premise is this: God has no favorite children. What has worked for me will also work for you. What brought power to the lives of men like Luther, Wesley, Finney and Moody can also bring you power. It does not matter if you are an ordained minister or a housewife. Your level of education or your station in life is of no consequence when it comes to prayer. If God has worked through men and women in the past, He can work through you.

One of the greatest lies of Satan is that we just don't have enough time to pray. However, all of us have enough time to sleep, eat and breathe. As soon as we realize that prayer is as important as sleeping, eating and breathing, we will be amazed at how much more time will be available to us for prayer.

As you read this book, please take time to pray about each chapter. What is contained in the following pages is more than just information. I have tried to give you more than mere formulas. What I have tried to share is based on twenty-seven years of experience in successful praying as I have seen prayer bring definite and precise results.

I have total and complete confidence in the Holy Spirit who has caused you to pick up this book. Thus I ask you to read on prayerfully.

Preface: The Life of Prayer

A

Christianity first came to Korea in a significant way. In the divine providence of God, it did not come as an imperialistic force; but, Christianity came through two godly American missionaries. So often, the beginnings of something seemingly affects its future development. So it was with the introduction of the gospel to Korea.

The signing of a treaty agreement between Korea and the United States in 1882 afforded a new "open door" for missionary work which the churches of America were anxious to enter. The Northern Presbyterian Board in 1884 transferred Dr. H. N. Allen from China to Korea. In 1885, the Rev. Horace G. Underwood, Presbyterian, and the Rev. H. G. Appenzeller, Methodist, became the first two missionaries appointed to Korea from the United States. These two men had a most significant impact on the future development of Christianity in Korea.

From the very beginning, the churches in Korea were national churches in that they were led, supported and developed by Korean ministers. Describing the success of this venture, Dr. Underwood wrote: "Very early in the history of the work, almost at its beginnings, God in His Providence led us to adopt methods that have been said by some to have been unique, but in reality are simply those that have been adopted by numbers of missionaries in different parts of the world. The only unique feature has been the almost complete unanimity with which these have been followed by the whole missionary body in this land."[1]

One of the most important aspects of our early church was that each morning the members gathered together for prayer. In 1906 revival broke out. Believers gathered in the Presbyterian church in Pyongyang, which is now the capital of North Korea. As they prayed, the Holy Spirit fell on them and they began to confess their sins. As a result, Koreans were converted in all parts of the country as the spirit of prayer prevailed.

When I began my pastoral ministry in 1958, I went to Dae Jo Dong, a poor area outside Seoul. I pitched a used U.S. Army tent and began to preach. I remember so well actually living in my tent, spending my nights in prayer. During our cold Korean winters, I would cover myself with blankets and spend many hours in prayer, lying near my pulpit. Soon, other members of my small congregation began to join me in prayer. In a short period of time, more than fifty people were gathering to spend entire nights in prayer. This is how I began my ministry.

It was during that formative period of my ministry that I learned the ministry of intercession. Although I will deal with that particular ministry of prayer later, it is important for us to understand that my intercession was first for my people, then for my nation and, last of all, for myself.

We have learned not only to pray, but we have learned how to live our lives in prayer. Jesus commanded us to pray without ceasing. To those not interested in revival, this is impossible. If your heart hungers for souls to be saved and your nation to be turned to God, however, then the life of prayer is a must.

Not only in our church, but in most churches in Korea, our

---

[1]Underwood, Lillias. *Underwood of Korea* (Fleming H. Revell, New York, 1918), p. 5.

prayer time begins at 5:00 A.M. We regularly pray for one or two hours. After our prayer time, we begin the normal routines of our day. Since the most important thing in our lives is prayer, we have learned to retire early. On Fridays, we spend the entire night in prayer. Many of our visitors are surprised to see our church packed with people for our all-night prayer meeting.

On Sundays, before each one of our seven services, we spend time in prayer. I am shocked when I visit churches that have social gatherings before Sunday services. More can be accomplished if each person comes to church in an attitude of prayer and quietly prays before the service. This is why the holy and mighty presence of God is in our services. Sinners are convicted by the Holy Spirit even before I get up to preach the gospel. Christian hearts are opened to receive the truth of God's Word by the spirit of prayer among us.

During our Sunday services, the believers pray together. The sound of thousands of Korean believers praying together reminds me of the thunderous roar of a mighty waterfall. "And I heard a voice from heaven, as the voice of many waters, and as the voice of a great thunder. . . ." (Rev. 14:2).

Visiting ministers who preach from my pulpit are struck by the power of the Holy Spirit sensed within our services. One American minister told me, "Dr. Cho, God is in this place. I can feel His presence." Then, tears streamed down his face as he said he had never before experienced the Holy Spirit's presence to that degree.

Originally, Prayer Mountain was land purchased for use as a church cemetery. However, during the construction of our present church on Yoido Island, when we were going through great trials, people began going there for prayer and fasting. Today, it is a "city of prayer" with a large auditorium that seats over ten thousand people. It also has several other prayer chapels. On the side of Prayer Mountain there are what we call "prayer grottos." These are dug right into the side of the hill and are used for complete solitude in prayer. I have my own prayer grotto which I often use. Many of the answers to problems that I have faced in our church have been solved in my prayer cell, at Prayer Mountain.

We have had as many as twenty thousand people fasting and praying at Prayer Mountain. Yet, normally, we have three thousand people during the week and ten thousand on weekends.

Why do so many people come to Prayer Mountain to fast and pray? Don't our Christians have better things to do with their time? My answers to these questions are simple and direct.

If you, or members of your family were dying of cancer, and you knew that there was a cure, wouldn't you do whatever was necessary to procure healing? Many people are suffering from both physical and spiritual cancer. Material prosperity has not brought the happiness and fulfillment that we once thought it would bring. The answer to physical and spiritual problems is healing. We have discovered that people's needs are met in a city totally dedicated to prayer and fasting. This is why they come.

Korean Christians trace their spiritual roots to America. We are also a loyal people. America delivered us from the great oppression of the Japanese and saved us from an invasion out of the Communist North. Thousands of Korean Christians therefore go to Prayer Mountain to pray for the thousands of prayer requests that come from the United States. People who watch our television programs in the United States, or anywhere else, rush their prayer requests to us. I personally pray for as many of them as I can, certainly the gravest ones. Then, once they have left my desk, they are brought up to our platform and put in a special place near my pulpit. On Sunday, more than three hundred thousand people will pray for those requests. The requests are then translated into Korean and sent to Prayer Mountain. Experienced "prayer warriors" are assigned to each request and they fast and pray until they get the witness of the Holy Spirit that their prayer has been answered.

A lady from Houston, Texas, wrote me, "You don't know what a help you are. To be able to lean on the faith God has given you is wonderful. I always write my prayer requests with tears for the burden God has placed on your heart for America. Please keep praying for us." Another person wrote me about knowing the exact time we were praying for her. "The healing took place when my prayer partner in Korea touched the Throne of God for my need." The testimonies are too many to mention in this section, but the results of the intercessory prayer at Prayer Mountain will only be known in eternity.

It is not easy for me to share my personal devotional life. Normally I keep these facts between my Lord and myself. But, to encourage you in prayer, I will tell you about my personal life of prayer.

I usually wake up between 4:30 to 5:00 in the morning. Of course, when I conducted our early morning prayer meetings at the church, I used to get up earlier. However, many of my associate pastors anxiously await their turn to lead our early morning prayer time, so I normally can stay at home very early in the morning.

I begin my personal prayer time by praising and thanking the Lord for the great blessing He is to me. I also praise Him for all He has done for my family. There is so much to praise Him for that just thanking and praising Him takes a good deal of time.

Then, I begin to intercede. I pray for our president and government officials. I pray for our nation so that the Angel of the Lord will protect us from the Satanic forces that wish to destroy our country. I remember my associates in the work of the Lord. I pray for the missionary programs that we are involved in, particularly the ones in Japan and the United States. My wife and three boys are then held up before the Lord in prayer. Before I know it, much of my prayer time has gone.

Not always knowing the needs of each person for whom I pray, I must trust the Holy Spirit to guide me. This is why a good deal of my time is spent praying in my spiritual prayer language. The Holy Spirit knows the mind of God and can discern the will of God for each individual and situation. If I pray in the Holy Spirit, then I know I will pray exactly according to the will of God.

Before I know it, my one hour is gone. After prayer, I am able to meet the challenges and opportunities that the day will present. Pastoring a church of over 370,000 members, and having an extensive international ministry, I am not able to do all that I have been called to do without spending the minimum of one hour in prayer every morning.

If I were to just get up and begin my days without spending the hours that I spend in prayer, I would only have my natural resources to depend on. Yet, having spent time in prayer, I can trust the unlimited resources at God's disposal.

During the day, I usually face many problems. Before I do or say anything, I pray. This is the difference between acting and reacting. As I study the life of Christ, I notice that Jesus always acted, and never reacted. To react is to allow people, situations or circumstances to be in control. To act is to be in control of the circumstances around you. Even when Christ was being judged before Pilate, the Roman governor, He was in control of the circumstances.

The way I keep from reacting is to discover the mind of God on each situation that presents itself to me. As I live my life in prayer, I know that I have the mind of Christ. Then, when I make a decision, I know it is the will of God and can stand firm in the assurance that I am acting for God.

In the afternoon, I get alone with my precious Lord and Savior, Jesus Christ, and spend time fellowshiping with Him. These days, it seems, He is drawing me more away from activity. He wants to spend more time alone with me. I know that if I satisfy His desire, He will allow me to have enough time to meet the duties that fall on me as pastor of the world's largest church. Sometimes, I hear His call in the middle of the day, and I must respond. I never know when I will be drawn away from my ministry to His people into my ministry to Him. However, I have set priorities on my time. Ministry to the Lord is before ministry to His people.

Before I step into my pulpit to preach, I must spend at least another two hours in prayer. If I go to preach in Japan, as I do every month, I must spend a minimum of three to five hours in prayer. Since I preach in the Japanese language, I am well aware of the great spiritual opposition which has kept back revival from Japan. Many don't realize it, but Japan has never had a revival. Out of one hundred and twenty million Japanese people, there are only a few hundred thousand Christians in the whole country. To bind the spiritual forces and get my heart ready for the ministry of the Word, I must spend all of that time in prayer. With this type of prayer life, I don't get to spend the hours of fellowship time with other Christians that I would surely enjoy. However, I must fulfill my calling as Christ's servant. To do this effectively, I must spend my life in prayer.

When I minister in America, I don't find the same spiritual opposition that I find in Japan, so I can afford to spend only two hours in prayer before preaching. In Europe, I spend only two to three hours in concentrated prayer.

I have had pastors and evangelists ask me how they can experience the same growth in their church as we are accustomed to in Korea. Yet, after meetings, they go out to eat and can spend many hours in fellowship. In the morning, they are too tired to pray. Having experienced this all over the world over many years, I decided to write this book. I hope that men and women of God will get serious enough about revival to get serious about their prayer life.

At the Yoido Full Gospel Church in Seoul, we teach our new converts about prayer. Yet, if I did not pray, they would not pray. Since most of our converts come to Christ through our twenty thousand cell groups, they can get personal teaching regarding the extreme importance of prayer.

I decided years ago that we could not take the revival that we are now experiencing in Korea for granted. Having studied church history, I realize that revivals must not only be prayed for to begin, but they must also be prayed for so that they may be maintained. Throughout the revivals the Western world has experienced, after several years, people begin to take the revival for granted. The way this happens is that they forget about the very thing that birthed the revival, prayer. Once continuous and fervent prayer is forgotten, the impetus of the revival is lost and all that is left is the momentum of the past.

What do I mean by the impetus and momentum of a revival? Driving an automobile is a perfect example of how these two principles work. Impetus is the force that is generated in a car when you step on the gas pedal. By applying this force, the auto will stay in motion. However, if you take your foot off the gas pedal, the impetus, or the force, will no longer operate; yet, the car still keeps moving. What causes the movement of the auto without the force? The movement is generated by momentum. The movement of a car under momentum is different than under impetus. The momentum of the car does not maintain movement, so that eventually the car will come to a halt.

When the Holy Spirit brings revival as an answer to prayer, the impetus of the revival must be maintained for there to be a continuation of that revival. If prayer is ever forgotten, the revival will move from impetus to momentum. Eventually, the special visitation of God will end up as a monument to the past.

In our church, we have committed ourselves to revival and church growth until the second coming of Jesus Christ!

In 1982, we led one hundred and ten thousand people to Christ. Out of these new converts, we were only able to absorb sixty thousand members. Therefore, we gave other evangelical churches a total of fifty thousand members.

In 1983 we had a total of one hundred twenty thousand new converts. Why are so many people being saved within a single church? We have seen the importance of developing and keeping a prayer life. If we stop praying, the revival will wane. If we continue praying, I believe that all Korea can be saved.

I believe that the same level of revival can be experienced in your church. There is no land too hard for the Holy Spirit to work. There is no church too dead. There is no country too closed to the gospel. The answer is prayer!

PRAYER:
KEY TO REVIVAL

Part I

Motivating Christians to Pray

1

What Prayer Accomplishes

△

Prayer Produces Power

God has created us in such a way that we need to know the purpose and benefit of something if we are going to be motivated to work for that thing. Although we may not like it, we are not able to change easily. If we actually realized the benefits of prayer we would have been praying before now.

Motivation works on the basis of desire. For someone to pray, he must learn to desire prayer. For him to pray as the Scriptures require, he must develop a great desire to pray.

How can you develop a great desire to pray? You must see the eternal and temporal benefits of prayer.

When we look in the Bible, we see powerful prayers. In the ministry of Moses, we see a man who had power in prayer. He could speak with authority not only to the enemies of God, but also to God's people. When he prayed, plagues came to Egypt. When he prayed, the Red Sea opened before Israel. Yet, how did Moses develop his prayer power? Moses developed a life of prayer.

Joshua saw the mighty hand of God work through his life and

ministry. He knew the will and strategy of God in battle. There-fore, mighty cities fell before the untrained army that he led. How did Joshua develop so much power with God? He had learned to pray. While Moses was praying in the mountain, Joshua spent the night at the foot of the mountain in prayer. When Moses departed, God had a trained leader who was famil-iar with prayer.

David was a man given to prayer. When he was anointed king of Israel, Saul was still on the throne. David could have been discouraged by the fact that only a few recognized his kingdom, yet prayer brought him to a place of trust. He waited for the Lord to place him on Israel's physical throne. David was strong enough in his relationship with the Lord that he did not kill Saul when he had the opportunity. After Saul's death, David's first action as the recognized king of Israel was to bring back the Ark of the Cove-nant to its rightful place at the center of Israel's worship. When we look at the power in the kingdom and life of David, we can see the source of his power, a life of prayer.

Elijah was the prophet of God during one of the worst times in the history of Israel. At that time, Israel had turned to the worship of Baal. Elijah prayed powerfully, challenging the prophets of Baal. When we remember the story of Elijah we think of his power, but we must see the source of that power. Elijah was a man of prayer. He would spend hours and even days in prayer. This is why when Elijah was taken up in the whirlwind by the chariot of fire, the sons of the prophets looked for him on the mountaintops of Israel.

However, no one has ever manifested the power of God like the Son of God, Jesus Christ. Before He entered His public ministry, He spent time with the Father in prayer. Jesus was known to have spent seasons of prayer with the Father alone. This was the source of His power. He could do nothing unless the Father revealed it to Him.

Are you tired of the powerless prayers that you hear coming from your lips? Are you ready for your church to enter into a powerful ministry in prayer so that your neighborhood, city or state knows the power that resides in your church? If this is your desire and you will do anything and pay any price, then get ready for God to dramatically change your life and ministry, bringing you into a new dimension of power.

There is no reason miracles shouldn't be taking place in your church regularly. There is no reason sinners should not be drawn to the Holy Spirit in your church. It has been reported to me that Charles Finney passed through a small community in upstate New York. Houghton, New York, was a normal town, yet one day as Charles Finney's train was passing by, the Holy Spirit fell on the sinners in the community. Men in cocktail bars fell on their knees under the conviction of the Holy Spirit and asked Jesus Christ to save them. If the Holy Spirit gave Charles Finney such power, should not He give us the same kind of powerful ministry? Finney rarely shared the key to his power; however, a reporter decided to spy on him. The newspaperman finally realized that the source of Finney's power was the hours that he spent in prayer.

I am convinced that in Korea we have seen just the beginning of the revival God has promised us. Although it is known throughout the nation that God is working in our church, we have not yet seen the power of God as we shall in the future if we are faithful.

The power of God is not only seen in healings, deliverances from evil spirits and massive conversions to Christianity; it is also seen in the open heaven that is over our country. What do I mean by this? When a country has an open heaven, there is a freedom and spiritual liberty in preaching the gospel. The level of faith is high and one does not find a great deal of spiritual opposition in a country that has an open heaven. In some countries, it is difficult to preach because there is so much spiritual opposition. Satanic forces that oppose the gospel are strong and there isn't much faith. This makes it difficult for those of us who minister the Word of God.

In Korea, I find it easier to preach than almost anywhere else When I preach the Word of God, sinners immediately respond for salvation. Why do we have this spiritual atmosphere? The answer is prayer.

Prayer not only produces corporate power, but it produces

individual power as well. I have learned, in my own personal ministry, that I must depend on the power of the Holy Spirit. It is not by might or natural power, but by the Holy Spirit that great things are accomplished for God. As I have learned to walk in the Holy Spirit, I have seen the power of God. How could I pastor a church of over 370,000 and still have time to travel all over the world almost every month in national Church Growth Conferences? How can I have enough time to have a television ministry on three continents? The answer is the power that comes from the Holy Spirit as I have dedicated my life to prayer.

People come to my office for prayer regularly. I have seen the lame walk, the blind see and the paralyzed leap from their wheel chairs by the power of God. Am I special? I said in my introduction that God has no special children. We can all have power in prayer if we are willing to pay the price.

To develop this kind of power in prayer, we must change our attitude. In the Gospel according to Matthew, Jesus made a revolutionary statement regarding the attitude necessary to produce spiritual power. Some approached Jesus regarding John the Baptist after he had been imprisoned. Jesus testified to the unique place of John the Baptist when he stated: "Verily I say unto you, among them that are born of women there hath not risen a greater than John the Baptist; notwithstanding he that is least in the kingdom of heaven is greater than he" (Matt. 11:11). How could a child of God who is in the kingdom of heaven become even greater than John the Baptist? In the next verse Jesus revealed the attitude necessary to develop spiritual power: "And from the days of John the Baptist until now, the kingdom of heaven suffereth violence, and the violent take it by force" (Matt. 11:12).[2]

It will take violent dedication to prayer to bring the power of God into our lives. This violent earnestness will be most evident in discipline. For power in prayer takes much time. For this

---

[2]Adam Clarke called the violence Christ referred to in Matthew: "The required violent earnestness" (Adam Clarke, *Commentary on the Holy Bible*, One Vol. Ed., Baker Book House, Grand Rapids, Mich.) p. 792.

reason we must set priorities for our time. Many things will crowd around us to keep us from spending the time necessary for developing power in prayer. By God's grace we are able to take the prize of power-packed prayer, if we have the proper attitude.

Prayer Brings Brokenness

Over the past twenty-five years I have learned that God cannot use a person who is not broken and completely surrendered to Him. When Jesus met Peter in his fishing boat, Peter had one reaction: he was convicted in his heart. He felt as if he were too sinful for Jesus to be in his boat. Having denied Christ three times, he was broken by the grace and forgiveness of Christ in giving him the opportunity to preach the first sermon in the church's history. As a result of Peter's ministry, three thousand came to Christ at the Day of Pentecost. Peter was also used by Christ to open the spiritual door to the gentile world. God was able to use Peter once he had been broken.

I have met many who are not serving the Lord today because of past sin in their lives. They may blame the pastor or some other Christian, but in their hearts they know that they have fallen short of the mark and have not learned. When a Christian makes a mistake, I always try to help him put his life together again. I explain that his mistake can be the means by which he can learn to be broken and humble before God.

A lack of brokenness causes a person who is used by God to become proud and arrogant. However, when a man is broken, his heart resists pride. Therefore, he can be used to a greater degree.

How does this take place in prayer?

When you come in contact with God in your time of prayer, the first thing you feel in your heart, as you enter into His divine presence, is a realization of your sin. No one can sense pride in the presence of a holy God. Once you sense your lack of natural qualifications to be in His holy Presence, you will begin to confess your sin and humble yourself before God. This does not mean that you don't belong before the Throne of Grace. In fact, the clear access has been paid for each believer by the blood of Jesus Christ. However, you realize that you have no natural qualifications to be there, and your immediate reaction is one of brokenness. Brokenness and pride cannot coexist!

Amazingly, as you enter into the Presence, you will be made aware of reactions, attitudes and actions that you may have forgotten. Just as Peter could not bear to have Christ in his ship because of the recognition of his sin, so also, you become aware of your great need before His holy Presence.

The next very natural reaction to the Presence is to desire to be forgiven for your sin. This is true in my own experience. I may have done some little thing without realizing it. However, as soon as I enter into my prayer time, the Holy Spirit will point to that very thing and I will need to be forgiven and set free. You might say that this is too hard. But you must remember, you now have a new desire to pray. You now also have a new attitude of violence against your own flesh and pride. You are learning how to walk softly and gently in the Holy Spirit. We will learn much more about this later in this book.

Yet, I must at this time emphasize the importance of walking gently with the Holy Spirit. For the Holy Spirit is a Gentleman!

Living your life before the Holy Spirit in gentleness, you will become accustomed to the Lord's abiding Presence. The Lord's continually abiding Presence will bring about two most important changes. The first is brokenness and the second is surrender.

Before we look in the Scriptures to see biblical examples of brokenness and surrender, I must share with you my personal experience regarding these two important attitudes.

God has never chosen to use perfect people to accomplish His perfect will. This is obvious in His choice of Jacob and King David. This is also obvious in His choosing me. My natural inclination is to want my own way. However, the ways of the Lord are not often my ways. So someone has to give in. Therefore, my role is to always give in to the Holy Spirit who has been given to me to lead and guide me into the ways of God.

The Holy Spirit is the Comforter. Yet, the Comforter can make you most uncomfortable if you are not willing to follow God's ways. How does the Holy Spirit insure your obedience to our Heavenly Father? By keeping us broken!

In order for someone to be broken, he must have first been whole. When the Lord chose David, he was whole within himself. He could have been a successful shepherd of his father's sheep. However, the Lord had more for him. He was to be the next king of Israel. But David would be more than just a king—he would also be a prophet. His prophecies would be the clearest sign of the future work of the Messiah. David would be more than a prophet and a king, he would also be a priest. None had ever been able to enter into the presence of God in the Tabernacle besides the High Priest. Yet, David was able to enter into the Holy Presence without dying. As prophet, priest and king, David was a perfect type of Christ.

As we look at the life of David, we see that he was capable of the most ugly and heinous sins. He was guilty of adultery and even murder. Although David paid for his sin, and is still paying because of the way people still point to his sin, he was stopped from pursuing his own way. This does not mean that any of us should commit sin in order to be broken. We cannot tempt the grace of God. However, the Holy Spirit, as we walk gently before Him, will keep an up-to-date account of our behavior. If we are to continue to walk in the Presence, we are to remain broken and humble.

To live like this is to walk in honesty before God and His people. In our Oriental custom, a leader should never be embarrassed before his people. The people don't want this and certainly the leader avoids it as well. This is what we call "losing your face." However, the Holy Spirit has overcome our natural customs and has caused me to be open and frank with my people. I remember wanting to die before I shared with my congregation something which I had done that had not been pleasing to God. Yet, this has built a trust between my people and me that has lasted more than twenty-five years.

In James we see this principle clearly, "But he giveth more

grace. Wherefore he saith, 'God resisteth the proud, but giveth grace unto the humble'" (James 4:6). Peter also states the same principle clearly: "Likewise, ye younger, submit yourselves unto the elder, Yea, all of you be subject one to another, and be clothed with humility; for God resisteth the proud, and giveth grace to the humble. Humble yourselves therefore under the mighty hand of God, that he may exalt you in due time" (1 Peter 5:5–6).

If we walk in a spirit of pride, then God resists us when we approach Him in prayer. If we are broken and contrite before Him, He gives us more grace. Success is based on the grace of God. We cannot do anything successful on our own merit, but by His divine grace we can do all things. What we need to be successful is more grace. How do we get more grace? We get it by being broken in humility before God.

The lesson of brokenness is not a popular one today. People only want to know how to be successful. Yet, I have learned that success does not come by learning easy formulas or principles: we must learn the secret of brokenness which gives us more grace. It is that grace that grants us ultimate success.

Job was a man who learned this lesson. "I was at ease, but he hath broken me asunder" (Job 16:12).

David, confessing his condition, having asked God's help and seeing His deliverance, said, "I am like a broken vessel" (Psalm 31:12).

Yet, the purpose of God is to break but not crush. If we break in an attitude of humility before God, we will not be crushed to pieces.

In Matthew, Jesus made clear the difference between being broken and being crushed. "Jesus saith unto them, 'Did ye never read in the scriptures, The stone which the builders rejected, the same is become the head of the corner: this is the Lord's doing, and it is marvelous in our eyes? Therefore, say I unto you, The kingdom of God shall be taken from you, and given to a nation bringing forth the fruits thereof. And whosoever shall fall on this stone shall be broken; but on whomsoever it shall fall, it will grind him to powder'" (Matt. 21:42–44).

In understanding brokenness before God we must understand the nature of the simile. Christ is shown as the cornerstone of the spiritual temple, the church. The church in this context is more than the body of believers that was brought into being at the Day of Pentecost. In this context, the church is representative of God's people from the beginning. At the time Jesus was speaking, as quoted in Matthew 21, God's people were being represented by the Jewish nation. Jesus Christ is listed as the most important part of the building in which every member is depicted as a stone. He is the cornerstone, or the stone that holds the entire building together.

God's desire was to have a spiritual building that could properly contain His glory. By rejecting the Messiah, Israel forfeited the right to be that spiritual building. Therefore, God is creating a new building in the church. Each of us is a living stone in the new spiritual temple. When we are taken from the world in salvation, we are stones which need to be shaped so that we can function according to the will of God. When building a stone building, the master builder spends a great deal of time shaping each stone to fit in its rightful place. If that stone is too hard to be fitted and refuses to be properly shaped, then that stone is of little value and is simply crushed to powder.

Jesus therefore could command, "Fall on the rock and be broken!" The breaking of God is not to annihilate us, but it is to shape us into a form that can be properly used for the purposes for which God originally chose us. If we resist the purpose of God, the result is crushing, or being good for nothing in God's eternal purpose.

Therefore, it is so important for us to walk in brokenness before God. Yet, I must reiterate that this does not mean walking in failure or poor self-image. Remember that God chose us. We are important. However, as we learn to move into the Holy Spirit's presence in prayer, the natural result will be a broken attitude that will allow Jesus Christ, the master builder, to complete His divine work in our lives.

What a joy it is for us to know that God is shaping our lives to be used for His eternal purpose. What a peace we have knowing that all things are working toward this eternal end. Nothing is an accident. Everything is working for our eternal good. Praise the living Lord!

After brokenness comes surrender. With a nonconditional surrender, there comes a total yielding to the will of God. I must emphasize here that this does not make us passive. Surrender means we give up our natural right to do what we want over to our new master, the King of kings and Lord of lords.

We must also realize that brokenness and surrender are not ends in themselves. They are simply means toward the end of being effective instruments in the hand of God to be used for revival and church growth. In the past the problem has been that people have settled for brokenness and surrender as an end and not as a means. This has led many people into monasteries to live out pious lives that do not change their surroundings. Piety should not lead us away from the world, but should strengthen us so that we can be effective witnesses in the world.

The easiest thing to do is to retreat from the challenges that the world brings to the church today. Yet, the purpose of God for breaking and causing us to surrender is to equip us to confront those challenges.

My church is only a few hundred yards from the Congress Hall. In our government, I am often asked to pray over many issues that affect the entire nation. I have not retreated from the social and economic challenges which the Lord has placed before me. However, I have tried to be broken and surrendered enough so that I might clearly know the mind of God in each situation and challenge. In this way, my predominantly non-Christian country can know the mind of God.

Prayer and Overcoming Satan

We are living in an evil age. Satan, supported by the fallen angels and demons, is out to rob and destroy. Without depending on the power of prayer, we are not able to break Satan's power.

The devil has never been too concerned about church ritual—but he is deathly afraid of genuine prayer. When you begin your life of prayer, you are going to discover new and diverse opposition from Satan.

A man of my church was once an alcoholic. Although he was a success in business, his drinking problem caused him to be abusive to his wife and family. One evening he brought home a number of his drinking buddies and began to have a party.

Although his wife loved her family and had endured a great deal from her husband, she could not stand the fact that her husband had brought such dishonor to her home. She called her husband aside and said, "Dear, I love you, but I cannot take your drinking. Now you are bringing these drunks home with you. I will not stand for it. I am going to pack my bags and leave. Tomorrow when you wake up, I shall not be here. Good-bye!"

Suddenly the shock of losing his family sobered him up. Knowing that she was a devoted Christian, he knelt before her and began to cry, "Lord, please deliver me from the terrible spirit of alcohol!" Believing that her husband was not only drunk but was now mocking her religion, she became even more indignant.

He had tried so often to be delivered from his habit, but to no avail. Now that his wife had threatened to leave him, he was even more desperate. As he wept he heard an internal voice coming from his heart, "You will be set free by morning."

"I know for sure that by tomorrow I will be totally delivered," he cried to his wife. The look of disbelief could not be hidden from her face. She had heard similar promises before. However, by morning she was surprised to see her husband throwing his expensive liquor and cigarettes into the garbage. "Could a miracle of deliverance really be taking place?" she asked herself.

Later, he got into his car, drove to work and told all of the employees in his factory that God had set him free and he would never drink or smoke again. The other people in the factory did not dare to laugh openly, but they figured this was just another story. He had done similar things before. Yet, after a while, everyone was convinced that something had happened when his life style was totally changed. His whole family is now serving Jesus and he has become a deacon in our church.

Satan was out to destroy another family. Yet, through persistence and prayer, his wife was able to see the total and complete victory. Satan is a liar and the father of lies. He loves to rob and destroy, but Christ has given us the authority over Satan's work as we learn how to pray.

To understand how prayer can bring down the power of Satan at work in our friends and loved ones, we must understand what the Scripture has to say about him.

Satan had access to God as the leader of the heavenly worship. Isaiah states, "How art thou fallen from heaven, O Lucifer, son of the morning! How art thou cut down to the ground, which didst weaken the nations! For thou hast said in thine heart, I will ascend into heaven, I will exalt my throne above the stars of God: I will sit also upon the mount of the congregation, in the sides of the north! I will ascend above the heights of the clouds; I will be like the most High. Yet, thou shall be brought down to hell, to the sides of the pit" (Isa. 14:12–15).

Ezekiel further states, "Thou hast been in Eden the garden of God; every precious stone was thy covering, the sardius, topaz, and the diamond, the beryl, the onyx, and the jasper, the sapphire, the emerald, and the carbuncle, and gold; the workmanship of thy tabrets and of thy pipes was prepared in thee in the day that thou wast created. Thou art the anointed cherub that covereth; and I have set thee so; thou wast upon the holy mountain of God; thou hast walked up and down in the midst of the stones of fire. Thou wast perfect in thy ways from the day that thou wast created, till iniquity was found in thee. By the multitude of thy merchandise they have filled the midst of thee with violence, and thou hast sinned; therefore I will cast thee as profane out of the mountain of God; and I will destroy thee, O covering cherub, from the midst of the stones of fire. Thine heart was lifted up because of thy beauty, thou has corrupted thy wisdom by reason of thy brightness; I will cast thee to the ground, I will lay thee before kings, that they may behold thee . . . . All they that know thee among the people, shall be astonished at thee; thou shalt be a terror, and never shalt thou be any more" (Ezek. 28:13–19).

Satan's former prominence in God's glorious heavenly realm is made clear from the preceding Scripture. Yet, why would he want to rob and destroy us?

God created man in His own image. He gave him dominion. Satan was jealous of man's place and has from the beginning tried to destroy God's special creation. After Adam and Eve died spiritually due to their sin, God made a promise: "And I will put enmity between thee (Satan) and the woman, and between thy seed and her seed; it shall bruise thy head, and thou shalt bruise his heel" (Gen. 3:15). Therefore Satan has known that through mankind, he would suffer his ultimate and final defeat.

Throughout the history of man, Satan has tried to keep this promise from coming to pass. He first tried to pollute the human race: "And it came to pass, when the men began to multiply on the face of the earth, and daughters were born unto them, that the sons of God saw the daughters of men that they were fair; and they took them wives of all which they chose. And the Lord said, 'My spirit shall not always strive with man, for that he also is flesh: yet his days shall be a hundred and twenty years.' There were giants in the earth in those days; and also after that, when the sons of God came in unto the daughters of men, and they bare children to them, the same became mighty men which were of old, men of renown. And God saw that the wickedness of man was great in the earth, and that every imagination of the thoughts of his heart was only evil continually. And it repented the Lord that he had made man on the earth, and it grieved him at his heart . . . . But Noah found grace in the eyes of the Lord" (Gen. 6:1–8).

Satan's trick was to pollute the human race so that the seed of woman (Jesus Christ) could not be pure. Therefore, He could not bring destruction to his kingdom. Yet, God had one man that had not been polluted. One family found favor in the sight of God. So Noah was the means by which the human race was saved from total and complete destruction.

Satan continued his opposition by trying to destroy Israel. Then, he tried to destroy the Christ child. Finally, he hung the Son of God on the cross. Yet, the cross was not the end, but through the death of our precious Lord on the cross, Satan was defeated by Jesus Christ. Because of the death and the resurrection of Jesus Christ, we also have been given authority over Satan and his works. Therefore we are more than conquerors through Him who loved us.

How is this authority exercised in prayer?

As I stated before, Satan opposes the prayers of God's people more than anything else. This is evident in the Book of Daniel.

Daniel was still a young man when he was taken captive by the Babylonians in 605 B.C. God allowed this captivity to be the means by which Daniel was given a key position in the greatest empire of that day. As Joseph found favor in Egypt, while experiencing temporary setbacks, so Daniel was used by God because of the gift given to him to interpret dreams. This gift was later used to show such a precise vision of the future that many scholars doubt the authenticity of the book.

In the first year of Darius the Mede, the future universal ruler of the Middle East, Daniel received special understanding of Jeremiah 25:12. As he realized the implications his new understanding had for Jerusalem he began his famous intercessory prayer for his people. He began by confessing his own sin, although his uncompromising faithfulness to God was recognized by all Jews in captivity. He then began to ask forgiveness for his people, as is seen in the ninth chapter. He continued by petitioning God for his people, "O Lord, according to all thy righteousness, I beseech thee, let thine anger and thy fury be turned away from thy city Jerusalem, thy holy mountain: because for our sins, and for the iniquities of our fathers, Jerusalem and thy people are become a reproach to all that are about us. Now therefore, O our God, hear the prayer of thy servant, and his supplications, and cause thy face to shine upon thy sanctuary that is desolate, for the Lord's sake" (Dan. 9:16–17). As he continued in prayer, his supplications became more impassioned, "O Lord, hear; O Lord, forgive; O Lord, hearken and do; defer not, for thine own sake, O my God: for thy city and thy people are called by thy name" (v. 19).

As Daniel continued in prayer, God sent the angel Gabriel to visit him. Gabriel then reveals the way Satan opposes the prayer of God 's people. "Then said he unto me, 'Fear not, Daniel: for from the first day that thou didst set thine heart to understand, and to chasten thyself before thy God, thy words were heard, and I am come for thy words. But the prince of the kingdom of Persia withstood me one and twenty days: but lo, Michael, one of the chief princes, came to help me; and I remained there with the kings of Persia' " (Dan. 10:12–13).

Later in the chapter, Gabriel shows the battle he will face when he leaves Daniel: "Then said he, Knowest thou wherefore I come unto thee? And now will I return to fight with the prince of Persia; and when I am gone forth, lo, the prince of Grecia shall come. But I will show thee that which is noted in the scripture of truth; and there is none that holdeth with me in these things, but Michael your prince" (vv. 20–21).

In Kiel and Delitzsch's *Commentary on the Old Testament*, one of the most respected commentaries on Scripture, the assertion is made that the Prince of Persia was the spiritual force that guided the advancement of the next world government. Gabriel had been sent by God, but the Satanic princes, or fallen angels, made war against Gabriel—Satan not wanting Daniel's prayer to be answered. Michael, the archangel, was called in to assist Gabriel in the battle. Daniel had fasted and prayed for twenty-one days. This was the length of time necessary for God's spiritual forces to overcome the fallen angels.[3]

In Zechariah 3 we see the angel of the Lord saying to Satan, "The Lord rebuke thee, O Satan, even the Lord that hath chosen

---

[3]Keil-Delitzsch, *Commentary on the Old Testament*, vol. IX (Wm. B Erdmans Publishing, Grand Rapids, Mich.) pp. 416, 417.

Jerusalem rebuke thee: is not this a brand, plucked out of the fire?" (v. 2).

Paul understood the spiritual warfare that we have been called to exercise when he stated, "For we wrestle not against flesh and blood, but against principalities, and powers, against the rulers of the darkness of this world, against spiritual wickedness in high places" (Eph. 6:12).

To put all of this into clear perspective we must understand the spiritual reality, or what I have called "the fourth dimension."[4]

Satan was cast down from his place in the heavenlies where he held an exalted position. We were created higher in stature than the angels, in that we are capable of understanding spiritual reality. Satan has known since the Garden of Eden that through mankind, his kingdom would be destroyed. God gave him the title: "prince of the power of the air" (Eph. 2:2). As he has been able to exercise real authority over the earth's atmosphere, he has been able to influence the nations. Yet, God gave man authority. Man lost the authority in the Fall through the sin of Adam. Yet, God has not been without a witness in the world. His people have been able to exercise authority in prayer and intercession. When Christ came, He allowed the world to judge and crucify Him. Yet, through His sinless life, atoning death on the cross and glorious resurrection, Christ took the keys of death and the grave and received "all authority" (Matt. 28:18). On the basis of the fact that Christ has won all the authority in heaven and on earth, we are therefore commanded to go into all the world and disciple nations to the kingdom of God.

As we learn how to pray in the Holy Spirit, realizing that we have been given the authority, we are able to bind the forces of Satan in people, communities and even in nations. However, because Satan is a liar and the father of lies, he tries to convince us that he is in control. But as we learn to fast and pray and exercise our rightful spiritual authority, Satan and his forces must yield to the will of God.

---

[4]*The Fourth Dimension*, vol. 2 (Bridge Publishing, Plainfield, New Jersey).

How important it is for us to know and understand the importance of prayer. There is no way we are going to see the will of God accomplished in our lives and ministry if we don't learn how to pray. Yet, as I stated earlier, we must first desire to pray.

Our problem has been that we have thought about prayer, read about prayer and even received teaching regarding prayer, but we just have not prayed. Now is the time to understand that prayer is the source of power. Now is the time to allow the Holy Spirit to bring a new brokenness and surrender. Now is the time to learn how to use our spiritual authority in learning how to hinder the work of the devil. Now is the time to pray!

2

Prayer and the Holy Spirit

△

This is the age of the Holy Spirit. Jesus told the disciples that it was imperative for Him to go away so that the Holy Spirit would come. At the Day of Pentecost, the Holy Spirit came upon and filled the 120 faithful who were waiting in Jerusalem. This was the fulfillment of the prophecy of John the Baptist.

At the baptism of Jesus Christ the Holy Spirit was symbolized as a dove. The purpose for the dove being the symbol is due to the nature and personality of the Holy Spirit. The dove is gentle and so is the Holy Spirit. You only really get to know the nature of the Holy Spirit as you begin to fellowship with Him. In the Old Testament, we don't see the Holy Spirit as a distinctive personality. In the New Testament, He so speaks of Christ, that one may miss the rich nature that is true of the Third Member of the Trinity.

How do we get to know the Holy Spirit? We only become aware of His nature as we enter a life of prayer.

Of all the Gospels, the Gospel according to John has the most references to the Holy Spirit. In the fourteenth chapter, He is called the Spirit of Truth and the Comforter. He is the Spirit of Truth in that He can take the words of Christ and reveal the depth of meaning that the Word contains. He is the Comforter in that He will bring into our hearts a peace that the world cannot give. The world only knows peace through the cessation of hostilities. The Holy Spirit brings peace irrespective of any circumstances. Therefore, as we learn to walk in the Holy Spirit, we learn to walk in truth and peace. If we don't have truth at work in our lives, if we don't walk in the peace of God, we are most likely not walking in the Holy Spirit.

Prayer Opens the Door for the Holy Spirit

The Holy Spirit can bless you when you read the Scriptures. The Holy Spirit can direct you as you witness for Christ. The Holy Spirit can anoint you as you preach and teach the Word of God. But if you want to have an intimate communion with the Holy Spirit you need to pray.

I first realized this truth in the early days of my ministry. I tried so hard to lead people to Christ, but with few results. As I was in prayer, the Lord spoke to my heart, "How many quail would Israel have caught if they had gone quail hunting in the wilderness?" I responded, "Lord, not too many." "How did the quail get caught?" the Lord continued to ask me. I then realized that God sent the wind which brought the quail. The Lord was trying to show me the difference between chasing souls without the Holy Spirit's strategy and working in cooperation with the Holy Spirit. Then the Lord said something to me that totally changed my life, "You must get to know and work with the Holy Spirit!"

I knew I was born again. I knew I was filled with the Holy Spirit. Yet, I had always thought of the Holy Spirit as an experience and not as a personality. However, getting to know the Holy Spirit would require my spending time talking with Him and letting Him talk to me. This fellowship with the Holy Spirit has brought me into every major change in my ministry. The development of the cell system came out of fellowship with the Holy Spirit in prayer. The founding of Church Growth International came out of fellowship with the Holy Spirit. In fact, every major principle that I teach in Korea and around the world did not come out of a theological book, but it came from genuine and intimate fellowship with the Holy Spirit in prayer.

In my personal life, fellowship with the Holy Spirit has made all the difference in the world. I could not live without that sweet communion with His presence that I have become so familiar with. In the morning, I can sense His freshness come over my heart and I have the strength to go through the challenges of that day knowing that in every situation I will be completely victorious.

I have also discovered that I am not smart enough to solve the thousands of problems that come to me regularly. Yet, I can just say to the Holy Spirit, "Sweet Spirit, please let me tell You about the problem I have. I know You know the mind of God and You already have the answer." With assurance, I then await the answer from the Holy Spirit.

Discovering throughout these many years that the Holy Spirit renews me spiritually, mentally and physically, I have seen that daily communion with the Holy Spirit is a necessity. Out of the one hour that I spend in prayer every morning, much of that time is spent in fellowship with the Holy Spirit.

Each time God gives me something fresh and new from the Word, I know that it comes from the Spirit of Truth who dwells within me. Just as the Holy Spirit caused Mary to conceive, so the Holy Spirit can impregnate us with the Living Word. "The letter killeth, but the Spirit giveth life." This is why so many thousands of people line up in front of our church on Sunday for each one of our seven services. This is why our televised service in Korea is one of the highest-rated programs. People are not just interested in being taught the Word, but they desire the Truth that is anointed by the Holy Spirit. Paul experienced teaching in this way. He testified to the church at Corinth, "Now we have received, not the spirit of the world, but the spirit which is of God; that we might know the things that are freely given to us of God. Which things also we speak, not in the words which man's wisdom teacheth; comparing spiritual things with spiritual" (1 Cor. 2:12–13).

The Holy Spirit not only anoints us to minister the Word of God with power and authority, but He also protects us from the attacks of Satan. Pastoring the largest church in the world does not free me from attacks from others. The attacks that come from the world do not bother me. It is the attacks which come from some of God's people that have the potential to hurt. Yet, daily communion with the Holy Spirit can shield us, not from the attacks, but from the effects of the attacks. In the life of Stephen, the church's first martyr, we see this principle clearly revealed.

Stephen proclaimed the Word of God with great power, as we read in Acts 7. Yet, Israel's response was only to be so convicted by his words that they desired to kill him. "When they heard these things, they were cut to the heart, and they gnashed on him with their teeth. But he, being full of the Holy Ghost, looked up steadfastly into heaven, and saw the glory of God, and Jesus standing on the right hand of God. And said, 'Behold, I see the heavens opened, and the Son of man standing on the right hand of God'" (vv. 54–56).

Paul closed his second letter to the church at Corinth by telling them, "The grace of the Lord Jesus Christ, and the love of God, and the communion of the Holy Ghost, be with you all." He again referred to the communion with the Holy Spirit in Philippians 2:1.

If your prayers are empty and not refreshing, it could be that you are not obeying the admonition of Paul and are not fellowshiping with the Holy Spirit. The Holy Spirit will bring you into the same joy, peace and feeling of right standing that you so desire. Remember that the kingdom of God is not meat and drink, but righteousness, peace and joy in the Holy Spirit.

Prayer Brings the Holy Spirit's Manifestations

In his first letter to the church at Corinth, Paul wrote, "Now concerning spiritual gifts, brethren, I would not have you ignorant" (1 Cor. 12:1). This verse could just as easily be written today. So much of the church is ignorant regarding the gifts and manifestations of the Holy Spirit. Of those who know about these gifts and manifestations, many do not know how and when to operate them.

The Holy Spirit first enters into a person when he is born again. After that, we are admonished to enter a more intimate relationship with the Holy Spirit. I call this "receiving the fullness of the Holy Spirit."

We enter this fullness through prayer. We also learn how to exercise our spiritual gifts through prayer.

The ministry gifts

Paul divides the ministry gifts in several scriptural references. These gifts are given as God chooses to give them, "But now hath God set the members every one of them in the body, as it hath pleased him" (1 Cor. 12:18). Once we know our ministry gift, we are to develop that gift. "Neglect not the gift that is in thee, which was given thee by prophecy, with the laying on of the hands of the presbytery. Meditate upon these things; give thyself wholly to them; that thy profiting may appear to all" (1 Tim. 4:14–15). In this last reference, Paul teaches Timothy that meditating, in prayer, will help develop the ministry gift given to him.

In 1 Corinthians 12, Paul lists, not exhaustively but essentially, the ministry gifts: Apostles, Prophets, Teachers. Then, he lists a lower but not less valuable level of ministry gifts: Miracles, Gifts of Healing, Helps, Governments and Languages.

The first level of ministry gifts is more exhaustively listed in the letter to the Ephesian church, "And he gave some, apostles; and some, prophets; and some, evangelists; and some, pastors and teachers" (Eph. 4:11). This first level of ministry gift is then told what their function is in the next verse: "For the perfecting of the saints, for the work of the ministry; for the edifying of the body of Christ" (v. 12).

What is the purpose of Christian Ministerial Leadership? It is to train lay people to minister so that the Body of Christ can be built and strengthened. How does a minister grow and develop his ministry? Through meditating on that ministry in prayer.

Therefore, whether you are a pastor or a church administrator, cell leader or deacon, your gift will only grow and develop through prayer and meditation.

The Holy Spirit's manifestations

Spiritual ministry gifts are given by the Holy Spirit in accordance with the Father's choice. Yet, every Christian can manifest the Holy Spirit. The purpose of the manifestation is that everyone in the assembly will be edified. Paul says, "But the manifestation of the Spirit is given to every man to profit withal. For to one is given by the Spirit the word of wisdom; to another the word of knowledge by the same Spirit; To another faith by the same Spirit; to another the gifts of healing by the same Spirit; to another the working of miracles; to another prophecy; to another discerning of spirits; to another diverse kinds of tongues; to another the interpretation of tongues: But all these worketh that one and the selfsame Spirit, dividing to every man severally as he will" (1 Cor. 12:7–11).

The fourteenth chapter of 1 Corinthians is dedicated to the proper use of the Holy Spirit's manifestation, particularly as regarding a public assembly. The main purpose of the manifestations is to build up the entire group and not just use the manifestation to prove individual giftedness or spirituality. The thirteenth chapter, better known as the "love chapter," does not say that love is better than spiritual gifts, but shows us the proper motivation for the exercising of these gifts. "But covet earnestly the best gifts; and yet show I unto you a more excellent way" (1 Cor. 12:31). Notice that Paul does not say, "I show you a more excellent thing." No. He is concentrating in chapter 13 on the "more excellent way."

Since God is a God of order, all things that are done in a church must also be in order: "For God is not the author of confusion, but of peace, as in all the churches of the saints" (1 Cor. 14:33).

As we teach Christians in Korea to pray that the church may be built upon a solid biblical foundation, the spiritual gifts addressed in 1 Corinthians are not ignored. The way to develop spiritual gifts and manifestations is to be dedicated to prayer. Prayer will cause the differing gifts of ministry to work together and not work in competition. Prayer will develop the motivation of love which will keep all spiritual gifts and manifestations in proper order. Prayer is the answer!

Prayer Creates Spiritual Sensitivity

Scripture is more than black ink on white paper. The words printed in the Bible are more than mere words. The words in the Bible are the Word of God.

"God is a spirit: and they that worship him must worship him in spirit and in truth" (John 4:24). Jesus said, "It is the spirit that quickeneth; the flesh profiteth nothing: the words that I speak unto you, they are spirit, and they are life" (John 6:63). Therefore, the Holy Spirit can bring us to such a spiritual sensitivity that we are able to understand God's Word in a new and greater dimension.

Paul also stresses this point, "But we speak the wisdom of God in a mystery, even the hidden wisdom, which God ordained before the world unto our glory: Which none of the princes of this world knew: for had they known it, they would not have crucified the Lord of glory. But as it is written, Eye hath not seen, nor ear heard, neither have entered into the heart of man, the things which God hath prepared for them that love him. But God hath revealed them unto us by his Spirit: for the Spirit searcheth all things, yea, the deep things of God" (1 Cor. 2:7–10).

Paul also stresses the importance of understanding God's Word under the anointing of the Holy Spirit that comes through prayer when he states, "But the natural man receiveth not the things of the Spirit of God: for they are foolishness unto him: neither can he know them, because they are spiritually discerned" (1 Cor. 2:14).

The reason the Word of God is not understood by the world, even with all its natural wisdom, is that the Word of God belongs to a higher dimension than just natural wisdom and understanding. It contains a spiritual dimension impossible to comprehend without the Holy Spirit.

One of my favorite hymns is William F. Sherwin's, "Break Thou the Bread of Life." In verse four he wrote:

> O, send Thy Spirit, Lord, now unto me,
> That He may touch my eyes, And make me see;
> Show me the truth concealed within Thy Word,
> For in Thy book revealed, I see Thee, Lord.

When I pick up the most precious material possession I own, my Bible, I pray to the Holy Spirit, "O, Holy Spirit, open my eyes so I may see the Truth of God in Thy Holy Word." What a joy it is to study the Word of God after prayer.

Faith comes by hearing and hearing by the Word of God, Paul wrote in Romans. God increases our faith as we develop hearing, or spiritual sensitivity. Our spiritual sensitivity comes by prayerfully studying God's Word.

Dependency on the Lord increases your spiritual sensitivity. I have learned that as I depend completely on the Lord, He always guides me and gives me spiritual understanding. Often this takes spiritual boldness. Yet, after prayer, as I launch out in faith, I get even more spiritual sensitivity. As my spiritual senses are developed, I can understand the "strong meat" of the Word of God. "But strong meat belongeth to them that are of full age, even those who by reason of use have their senses exercised to discern both good and evil" (Heb. 5:14).

The writer to the Hebrews is simply showing the qualifications necessary to be able to eat strong spiritual food from the Scripture. Those who have developed their spiritual sensitivity, by using the discernment they already have, can take strong food.

Those who have not developed their spiritual sensitivity can only partake of the milk of God's Word.

One night, during our family's devotions, one of my sons said something that articulated the importance of my totally depending on the Holy Spirit. My oldest son told my wife, Grace, "Mother, I'm not going to spend so much time praying like Father does. I'm young and self-confident. I don't need to pray like he does. Why should I ask God to help me with everything? I can do a lot of things myself."

As I was hearing his words, my heart was struck with compassion for my teenage son. So I was very honest with him.

"Hee-jeh," I said, "you and your brothers look at your father and listen well," I continued. "Everyone in Korea knows your father. Is that correct?"

"Yes," they responded.

"Your father is now the pastor of the largest church in the world. Is that correct?"

"Yes, that is correct, Father," they agreed in unison.

"Now, look at your father! Once I was dying of tuberculosis. No doctor could help or cure me. Also, your father was so poverty-stricken he could not afford to go to the hospital to receive treatment. Your father's formal education stopped after his first year of high school. He has no high social position; no famous genealogy; and as a common person he has nothing to brag about. You have no natural thing to brag about your father. He has no money, position, or education. Yet, as I have depended on the Lord, look what He has done for me. But you know the secret to my success? I poured my heart out to the Lord. I depended upon Him. By the help of God, I educated myself. I read every book that came into my possession. I studied diligently, praying all the way. Now, by the grace of God, I am what I am.

"Sons, if you just depend on your own strength, education and natural wisdom; you will sink into the mire of this world. Do not be arrogant! Learn to depend on the Lord as I do!"

After speaking to my sons in this manner, I had assurance that they not only heard me, but they understood the implications of what I was saying. Their attitude changed as much as their countenance, after realizing the importance of total and complete dependence on the Lord.

As I pray, my sensitivity not only is exercised in Scripture, but also in discerning the Lord's presence. At times, God's presence is so near during my times of prayer and fellowship that I feel Him close enough to touch. How refreshed I feel after spending time with my precious Lord. The Christian life, particularly if you are in the pastoral ministry, can become dull and routine if you don't have this type of fellowship in prayer.

If you are not accustomed to this type of fellowship, the time to begin is now. Right now, put this book down and begin to ask the Holy Spirit to make the presence of Christ real to you! Ask Him to give you a new understanding of His Word. Ask Him to bring you into a new walk of fellowship in the Holy Spirit!

Shakespeare. However, there exists a piece of literature that is more important than all of the rest of the cumulative human literature in existence. This piece of literature is not static but is constantly expanding. It is continuously being written by God.

"Then they that feared the Lord spake often one to another: and the Lord hearkened, and heard it, and a book of remembrance was written before him for them that feared the Lord, and that thought upon his name. And they shall be mine, saith the Lord of hosts, in that day when I make up my jewels; and I will spare them, as a man spareth his own son that serveth him" (Mal. 3:16).

God has written and is writing a book called "the book of remembrance." Those who spend time thinking, or meditating, will find that God is keeping an accurate record. You and I can only imagine the richness of the spiritual thoughts special men have had about God all these years. We appreciate the beauty of the Psalms David wrote as he contemplated his relationship with God. Yet, what about the thoughts which were never written?

In the New Testament we read about the Book of Life. Paul in Philippians and John in the Book of Revelation speak about the importance of being named in the Lamb's Book of Life. Christ, the Lamb of God, is keeping accurate records of the redeemed.

What is most basic about the literature that God is writing is that it shows that God keeps spiritual records. Nothing is lost or wasted. Nothing that is done for Him is ever in vain. So often, we forget what people do for us. I have often said that those things people do for us are written on water, quickly disappearing. However, those things people do against us are written in tablets of stone, often remembered.

It is extremely important for us to remember that one never forgets, except for sins that are forgiven and are placed under the blood of Jesus Christ. Therefore, our prayers are remembered.

Persistence in prayer is important when you think in terms of accounting. We don't know how long we have to pray before God will answer our prayers. Daniel discovered that his prayer helped Gabriel in overcoming the spiritual opposition he encountered for twenty-one days. God heard the prayers and they were held in account.

In Luke 11, we can read Christ's response to the disciples' request: "teach us to pray." In giving the disciples the answer to their request, Christ tells a story. A friend is approached regarding the loan of three loaves of bread. The request is made in an inopportune moment as he has already retired for the evening. However, the urgency of the request causes the requester to persist. Jesus then said, "yet, because of his importunity, he will rise and give him as many as he needeth" (Luke 11:8).

Some prayers require a great deal of repetition for there to be a response. Whether because of spiritual opposition or some other reason, we are told to keep on praying.

Never give up praying for a need! What would have happened if Daniel had given up after only five or ten days? Remember that God is faithful! He will hear your prayers! He will answer as you pray and faint not! Allow the balance sheet of prayer to be heavily in your favor.

A lady in our church had a daughter who was not living a Christian life. It seemed that the more she prayed, the more her daughter would follow her worldly friends. Then, she heard me speak on this subject. The mother began to pray faithfully for her daughter and did not get discouraged because of the worsening circumstances. One day, as she prayed, she knew in her heart that the account was large enough to take care of the spiritual need before her. She had a witness in her inner being that God had done the work. Within a few days, the daughter came to church and gave her heart to the Lord. Now both of them are faithfully serving Christ.

Prayer Brings Health

For all the advancements of modern medical science, people are still suffering from sickness and disease. Doctors now say that heart disease and cancer are the greatest killers. They also agree that most of our physical problems are caused by stress.

People are afraid of nuclear destruction and annihilation. The pressures of modern life have affected the entire world, even in the most remote regions. What can help twentieth-century man overcome the stress and anxiety that plague him?

The answer to this question is not new but it is extremely neglected in today's society. The answer is prayer!

Paul wrote to the church at Philippi, "Be careful for nothing; but in every thing by prayer and supplication with thanksgiving let your requests be made known unto God. And the peace of God, which passeth all understanding, shall keep your hearts and minds through Christ Jesus" (Phil. 4:6–7).

We have a choice as Christians. We can either be anxious or we can trust in God. We can have our hearts and minds full of the cares of this world, or we can pray. What is the benefit of the latter?

Prayer deals with the cause and not just with the effects. If the cause of most of our illnesses is anxiety, then the way to deal with the symptoms resulting from anxiety is to handle the cause; that is, getting rid of anxiety.

Paul tells the Philippians the secret to living without anxiety. The secret is prayer. When you pray, you are placing the problem that has made you anxious in God's hands. Then, through thanksgiving, you leave the problem in God's hands and don't pick up the problem again. By dealing with the anxiety, most of the symptoms can simply disappear in time.

The result of this kind of living will produce a peace that passes or surpasses all natural understanding. Because now you are relying on your eternal resources, your Heavenly Father, you don't have to be fearful, you can be at peace. People in the world won't understand this because it seems foolish to them.

Today, men feel that they must do everything for themselves. We have become the "I'll do it for myself" generation. The last thing the world wants to do is trust in anyone else, especially God. Because of this, they are suffering with stomach ulcers, heart attacks and cancers more now than ever. Yet, we can live our lives full of great peace. We have to give our problems to the Lord in prayer. We can therefore live healthy lives.

The purpose of this first section was to motivate you to begin praying as you have never prayed before. You have always known you needed to pray, but you just couldn't get enough time. You were always too busy.

Why should I write this book about prayer if it was not going to get you interested in praying? I did not need to spend the many months writing if you were just going to read it and return to your former ways. So the Lord directed me to share with you several things that would motivate you to pray.

You saw how prayer produces power in our lives. You realized that we needed more power to deal with the new and more complex attacks of Satan that he is using today.

Together, we traced the reason behind the devil's attack upon God's people. We also saw the way to overcome the attacks of Satan.

Prayer produces spiritual understanding. By praying, your whole life will be more aware of spiritual reality than ever before.

Also, prayer is the door for a more intimate fellowship with the Holy Spirit. We only learn how to move in our gift as we learn to pray. Each one of us has been given a spiritual gift that we must learn how to use. Prayer is the way to learn.

We looked at the account balance that can be built through prayer. Through persistent praying, our prayers will be answered.

Prayer is the key to our maintaining physical health! What a blessing it is not to need healing because you are healthy.

We are all designed to desire those things that we perceive are in our best interests. To motivate you to pray, I showed you how you could benefit from prayer in spirit, soul and body.

Now, you are ready to enter into the next section of this book: The Three Types of Prayer. In this next section you will see the three differing kinds of prayer and how to move in them successfully.

If you don't understand how prayer is divided, you may not understand all the Scripture that deals with prayer.

Why should some prayers get answered quickly and others take so long? Why should we ask God for things that He already knows we need?

The answers to these and other important questions will be addressed in the next section!

Part II

The Three Types of Prayer

Introduction

△

To understand the three types of prayer, we must see them in context within the teachings of Christ. No other place in the Gospels are these types of prayer made clearer than in the Gospel of Luke chapter 11.

"And it came to pass, that, as he (Jesus Christ) was praying in a certain place, when he ceased, one of his disciples said unto him, 'Lord, teach us to pray, as John taught his disciples.' And he said unto them, 'When ye pray, say, Our Father which art in heaven, Hallowed be thy name. Thy kingdom come. Thy will be done, as in heaven, so in earth. Give us day by day our daily bread. And forgive us our sins; for we also forgive every one that is indebted to us. And lead us not into temptation; but deliver us from evil.' And he said unto them, 'Which of you shall have a friend, and shall go unto him at midnight, and say unto him, Friend, lend me three loaves; for a friend of mine in his journey is come to me, and I have nothing to set before him? And he from within shall answer and say, Trouble me not: the door is now shut, and my children are with me in bed; I cannot rise and give thee . . . . And I say unto you, Ask, and it shall be given you; seek, and ye shall find; knock, and it shall be opened unto you'" (Luke 11:1–9).

What has commonly been referred to as "The Lord's Prayer" is also stated in another context in Matthew 6. However, in Matthew Christ is commenting on the motivation for prayer, not on the types of prayer. In Matthew, Christ teaches us to be careful that we don't practice our piety before people so that they admire us; on the contrary, we should only concern ourselves in prayer with the admiration of our Heavenly Father.

The context of Luke 11 sets the stage for the entire definitive teaching on prayer. Jesus had entered a favorite location in which He had dear friends. Bethany was a small town on the Mount of Olives, just outside Jerusalem. Mary, Martha and Lazarus, whom Christ later raised from the dead, resided in Bethany. Simon the leper, in whose home Christ was to be anointed, also resided in Bethany. When Christ made His triumphant entry into Jerusalem, He spent the night in Bethany. It was from just outside Bethany that the Lord was taken up into heaven. Needless to say, all of us have places where we can feel relaxed. I believe that Bethany was that type of place for our Lord.

Christ probably went into the garden at the back of the house to pray that evening. The disciples watched the special way in which Christ prayed and they desired to have the same kind of prayer life that Christ had. So they asked Him, "Lord, teach us to pray."

As a pastor, I have learned from the beginning of my ministry that the only way to cause my members to want to pray is to pray myself. If I did not have a life of prayer, I would not have a praying church, and I certainly would not be in the midst of revival. Christ's disciples were only ready to be taught how to pray after they had expressed the desire to learn because of His example.

In our Lord's teaching, He did not just give them a prayer formula; He gave them the basic principles of prayer. He taught them that prayer should begin with praise: "Hallowed be thy name!" He also taught them that prayer should have expectation: "Thy kingdom come. Thy will be done!" Prayer should also have petition: "Give us this day our daily bread." Confession should also be an integral part of prayer: "Forgive us our sins." Trusting in God's protective ability was also explained when He said:

"Don't allow us to come into the place of testing, but deliver us from evil" (my paraphrase from the original text).

The three types of prayer are listed in the ninth verse. They are pictured as three promises. Ask, and you will receive! Seek, and you will find! Knock, and the door will be opened!

In dividing the Word of Truth, the Scriptures, one can err by becoming too distinctive. Certainly there is overlapping when we study prayers of petition, devotion and intercession. Yet, the distinctions are apparent in Luke 11.

4

Prayer Is Petition

△

In prayer, we must learn to ask! Although it is true that God knows everything, we cannot develop the attitude that there is no need to ask anything from God because He already knows what we need. Some have come to the conclusion that we should not ask because of the verse found in Matthew: "Be not ye therefore like unto them; for your Father knoweth what things ye have need of, before ye ask him" (Matt. 6:8).

However, the context of the verse just quoted is most important in understanding the verse. Jesus had first said: "But when ye pray, use not vain repetitions, as the heathen do: for they think that they shall be heard for their much speaking" (Matt. 6:7). Therefore, repeating the same prayers ritualistically was what Jesus was referring to. He did not intend for us not to ask, as we shall see later; but, on the contrary, He intended us to ask our Father with prayers that proceed from our heart.

Petitioning God is basic to prayer! God is our Father; and as a father, He enjoys giving to His children. A child has rights in a family. God's Son, Jesus Christ, commanded us in strong language, "Verily, verily, I say unto you, Whatsoever ye shall ask the Father in my name, he will give it you. Hitherto have ye asked nothing in my name: ask, and ye shall receive, that your joy may be full" (John 16:23–24).

In verse 27, Christ shows why this works: "For the Father himself loveth you, because ye have loved me, and have believed that I came out from God." The Father loves us because we believe in His Son. Therefore, we are partakers of the inheritance of the only begotten Son of God.

God is a good God! He desires to give all good things to us if we just ask Him. "If ye then, being evil, know how to give good gifts unto your children, how much more shall your Father which is in heaven give good things to them that ask him?" (Matt. 7:11).

Christ came to this world to bring redemption and restoration to fallen man. When Christ hung on the cross, the Father was bringing about the conditions through which mankind could be restored unto complete fellowship with his God. Paul stated: "To wit, that God was in Christ, reconciling the world unto himself, not imputing their trespasses unto them; and hath committed unto us the word of reconciliation" (2 Cor. 5:19). Based upon the reconciling work of the Father, we all have the potential for salvation. Yet, salvation must be preached throughout the ends of the earth, giving all men the opportunity to accept or reject the gospel—the Good News that the price has been paid and direct access to God is available to all men. Yet, mankind has to ask and receive this great blessing of salvation. A man must ask Christ to forgive his sins through repentance. He must ask Christ to enter his heart. Although the gift of salvation is there for everyone, it can only be appropriated by asking.

Not only is our regeneration the product of asking for what was purchased for us; but, also, the Holy Spirit's fullness is available simply by asking, "How much more shall your heavenly Father give the Holy Spirit to them that ask him?" (Luke 11:13). Therefore, the gift of salvation, the fullness of the Holy Spirit, as well as all other gifts are available through petitioning prayer.

James states that God will not refuse anyone who asks God for wisdom, but will give it freely—as long as it is asked in faith (see James 1:5). The gifts of the Holy Spirit are available for the asking.

Healing, deliverance, prosperity and blessing are all to be asked for. We also have a right to ask for revival, "Ask ye of the Lord rain in the time of the latter rain; so the Lord shall make bright clouds, and give them showers of rain. . ." (Zech. 10:1). The blessing of God is ours for the asking. We can have God's blessings, typified in Zechariah as rain because God has commanded us to ask for them.

It becomes obvious that God is willing to give to His children; however, we must participate actively in the answer to our needs by asking.

How does asking work? How can we get our prayers of petition answered?

There are four conditions that must be met to get assurance that our petitions as Christians will be answered affirmatively:

1. We must ask in faith! Simply asking God for things will not assure you of a positive response. "And all things, whatsoever ye shall ask in prayer, believing, ye shall receive" (Matt. 21:22).
2. We must abide in a relationship with Christ! "If ye abide in me, and my words abide in you, ye shall ask what ye will, and it shall be done unto you" (John 15:7). When we abide in prayer, we develop spiritually so that His desires are ours; therefore, this spiritual blank check can be entrusted to us.
3. We must be motivated properly! "You ask and do not receive, because you ask amiss, that you may spend it on your pleasures" (James 4:3, NKJV). It is God's desire to give us all good things, we know that. Yet, so many requests are generated by sheer selfishness. God desires that what we ask should be to the end that He may be glorified.
4. We must ask in accordance with the will of God! Does this mean that we should wonder whether God wants us healed before we pray for healing? No! This is why knowledge of Scripture is so important. The Bible tells us what the will of God is. So, when we ask for something that God has promised us, then we know with certainty that we are praying in

God's will: "Now this is the confidence that we have in him, that if we ask anything according to his will, he hears us. And if we know that he hears us, whatever we ask, we know that we have the petitions that we have asked of him" (1 John 5:14–15, NKJV).

How does God answer our petitions?

God responds to our requests within the framework of His personality. That is, He does not just give us exactly what we need; on the contrary, He gives to us in abundance: "But my God shall supply all your need, according to His riches in glory by Christ Jesus" (Phil. 4:19, NKJV). God's resources are unlimited resources. In this way, He supplies all of our needs. Therefore, God is not lacking in any good thing. He has a storehouse full; if we would just learn how to open the storehouse, by knowing how to petition.

I learned these principles in the early days of my ministry. I studied the Scripture and discovered that God is a good God. During the most difficult economic depression after the Korean War, I began my ministry in the poorest area. I learned how to fast—not because I was spiritual, but because I had nothing to eat! Yet, through prayer and Bible study, I discovered that God is not just the God of America and Europe; God is the God of anyone who will learn to trust Him.

I have told this story many times, but I am always surprised at how many have never heard it. Yet it perfectly illustrates the way to get your petitions answered from our Father.

In the beginning of my ministry, I was still single; therefore, I lived in a small room. In the winter, I would wrap blankets around myself because I had no heat. Preaching the things that I was seeing in the Scripture concerning God's abundance, I found myself in a predicament. If God was so good, if He had such great and abundant resources, why was I so poor? This is a question which many, especially in the developing world, are still asking.

I decided I needed three things. Since I had no way to visit my members, I needed a bicycle. Having nothing on which to place my Bible, I really needed a desk. To go with the desk, I decided to ask for a chair. These three items seem very small to us today; but twenty-five years ago these items were very rare in our area.

However, in complete confidence, I asked my Heavenly Father for the three items: a chair, a desk and a bicycle. Month after month, I repeated these petitions to God, feeling that by continually requesting the same thing, He would finally hear and answer me. Yet, after six months, I became discouraged. "God, I know time means nothing to you. Yet, I really need these things now. Perhaps you plan on taking much longer in answering my request. But, if you wait too long, I'll be dead and won't need them," I prayed despondently.

Then, I heard a still small voice within me, "Son, I heard you the first day you prayed six months ago."

"Well, why didn't you give them to me?" I asked.

"You asked me for a bicycle. Right?" God continued. "However, there are many makes of bicycles. Which kind do you want? There are also different desks made out of different kinds of wood. What kind of desk do you want? There are also a number of makes and kinds of chairs. What kind of chair do you want?" Those words, spoken to me that night, totally revolutionized my life.

I decided to ask God for three specific items: A bicycle made in the U.S.A. At that time, I had three choices of bicycles, but the American one was the sturdiest. I asked for a desk made from Philippine mahogany. Finally, I asked for a chair; but not just any chair; this one had little wheels on the bottom, so I could wheel around my room like a "big shot." Within two weeks, I was given an American bike, slightly used by the son of an American missionary. I had my desk, made from mahogany wood from the Philippines, and a chair to go with my desk. Of course, it had the little wheels.

The amusing part of this story took place before God's provision came. One Sunday, I preached on Romans 4:17, "As it is written, I have made thee (Abraham) a father of many nations. Before him whom he believed, even God, who quickeneth the dead, and calleth those things which be not as though they were." During my sermon, I heard myself saying, with great assurance, "I have been given a bicycle, chair and desk!" I then went on to describe each item.

Three young men, who are now in the ministry, asked me after the service, "Pastor, can we see these three great gifts God has given you?" Understandably, they were curious because any one of those things would be considered unusual possessions in that area.

On the way home, I found myself fretting over what I was going to say to those young men when they saw an empty room. As I opened the door, I saw them looking around the barren little room for the bicycle, chair and desk. "Pastor?" one of them finally asked. "Where are they?" he continued, looking very perplexed.

"Right here!" I exclaimed, pointing to my stomach. "Where?" they all asked.

"Yes, right here!" I said, again pointing to my stomach.

"Let me explain by asking a question," I calmly continued, amazed at my own answer. "Where were you before you were born?"

"In my mother's womb," finally one answered me.

"Correct! Now, did you exist before you were born?" I asked them, seeing a glimmer of light now begin to shine in their faces.

"Yes, naturally we existed in our mother's womb."

"But no one could have seen you," I smiled, as I told them what they finally realized was my condition.

"Yes, I'm pregnant too! I am pregnant with a chair, desk and a bicycle that is made in America!" I proudly exclaimed, now seeing the look of surprise on their faces turn to laughter. "Well, Pastor. So, you are pregnant!" They said, laughing out loud.

I tried to caution them not to tell anyone about it; but, something like a man being pregnant could not be kept quiet. Word spread throughout the entire neighborhood that the pastor of the local church was pregnant. Women would look at me and smile as I walked by. Little children would put their hands on my stomach to feel for the bicycle.

Yet, when God miraculously provided for each item, I was the one who was smiling. In this way, God taught me to be specific in my petitions. This is how to pray in faith. Do not pray in generalities! Know what you need and write it down! Tell God in detail exactly what you are asking for! Then, begin to confess that you have received it! You may not want to do it in public, but begin to thank God and confess the answer! Remember that what we ask in faith, God will provide.

It has been significant for God to teach this to a pastor from a small country. Usually, only Western preachers talk about God's abundance in providing for their needs. But I can testify that God can do the same for any man or woman who will petition God according to His holy Word.

So often our sociological and economic conditions dictate our faith level. This is why it is so important for us to ask God to increase our visions and dreams, which are the language of the Holy Spirit. By having a greater vision we can see the greater provision of God.

Winston Churchill once said that great men must come from great countries, live in great times, and perform great tasks. This is normally true. However, Jesus Christ, the Son of God, came from a small and weak country, Israel. At the time of our Lord's coming, Israel was under the oppression of the Roman Empire. Although He performed the greatest of tasks, He certainly did not live in a great time for Israel. Yet He is the focal point of human history.

No matter who you are, you can make a difference! Your life can change your nation and the world—if you know the secret of petitioning prayer.

Solomon said, "A man's gift maketh room for him, and bringeth him before great men" (Prov. 18:16). God desires to give you much more than you can dream or imagine. Ask God for the gift that will cause you to have the greatest effect on your situation! Do not be satisfied with the status quo! I came from a poor home; from a poor country; and from poor natural circumstances. Yet, I have never had to force my way before great men (in the eyes of the world). The gracious gift that God has given me has brought me before kings, queens, presidents and many notable world leaders.

If God can do this for me, He can do this for you too! Even if you are reading this book in a poor Latin American country, your life can make an imprint on that country and the whole world. No matter in what location you find yourself, God may desire to use you in great revival fires that will sweep Africa, Asia or Europe. Ask, and you will receive!

5

Prayer Is Devotion

A

God told Moses, "But if from thence thou shalt seek the Lord thy God, thou shalt find him, if thou seek him with all thy heart and with all thy soul" (Deut. 4:29).

Man has been created to desire communion with God. There is a void that cannot be filled by anything but genuine communion with God. No matter what man acquires, it cannot replace the fellowship that fulfills the very essence of man's being—giving purpose to life, nourishing the core of his soul.

God created Adam and gave him the breath of life. He was a physical being before he was a spiritual being. Adam's spiritual dimension gave him the capacity for communion and fellowship with God in the midst of the garden, in the cool of the evening. Man lost his ability through sin. But God still desired to fellowship with man, so He took the initiative with Abram. Abram became the father (Abraham) of the faithful who would have the opportunity to fellowship with God.

Then God revealed His physical presence on earth in the Tabernacle of Moses. However, with few exceptions, only the High Priest could enter into the third part of the Tabernacle of Moses which was called the Holy of Holies

When David was finally recognized as king of Israel, his first act was to bring the Ark of the Covenant, the symbol of God's presence, back to the center of Israel's worship. However, rather than place it in Moses' tent, God requested that he erect one in Zion, the place where David had his personal home: "For the Lord hath chosen Zion; he hath desired it for his habitation" (Psa. 132:13). In Zion, God would have direct access and communion with Israel.

However, the worship of Israel again became the object of ritual. God again took the initiative to restore fellowship with man when He came in the person of Jesus Christ.

In the Church Age, we have been given the Holy Spirit to lead us into fellowship and communion with the Father and Son. Jesus said, "He shall glorify me: for he shall receive of mine, and shall show it unto you. All things that the Father hath are mine: therefore said I, that he shall take of mine, and shall show it unto you" (John 16:14–15). Jesus further amplifies: "And he that loveth me shall be loved of my Father, and I will love him, and will manifest myself to him" (John 14:21). Then in the twenty-third verse He said, "If a man love me, he will keep my words: and my Father will love him, and we will come unto him, and make our abode with him."

Petitioning prayer is important in getting what we need from God, but there is more to prayer than asking. Jesus said, "Seek and ye shall find!" God is not just a resource center from which we can get everything we need, no matter how noble our motives. He is a living being who seeks our fellowship: "But the hour cometh, and now is, when the true worshippers shall worship the Father in spirit and in truth; for the Father seeketh such to worship him" (John 4:23).

Therefore, the next level of prayer beyond "asking" is "seeking." This in no way discounts asking. The greater does not discount the lesser, but the lesser is always included in the greater!

The apostle Paul lived his life in communion prayer with Christ. To the church at Philippi he testifies: "But what things were gain to me, those I counted loss for Christ. Yea doubtless, and I count all things but loss for the excellency of the knowledge of Christ Jesus my Lord: for whom I have suffered the loss of all things, and do count them but dung, that I may win Christ" (Phil. 3:7–8). How could Paul win Christ? Remember that salvation is the gift of God, by faith, through grace. What Paul is referring to in Philippians 3 is more than receiving Christ in salvation, it is coming into a deep fellowship and communion. This type of prayer is not given freely, it must be sought after, thereby requiring effort. What did Paul receive from this type of prayer? He gives the answer in the tenth verse: "That I may know him, and the power of his resurrection, and the fellowship of his sufferings, being made comformable unto his death." And again, "I press toward the mark for the prize of the high calling of God in Christ Jesus" (v. 14).

In the fifteenth verse, Paul challenges all of us: "Let us therefore, as many as be perfect (mature), be thus minded . . . ." Paul reveals in this last verse that the sign of spiritual maturity is to desire to attain the spiritual level whereby we enter an intimate fellowship and communion with Christ. God is love. Love requires satisfaction through fellowship and communion. Therefore, God's very nature requires what we have been privileged to have the ability to give Him—communion.

Before 5 A.M. every morning, I don't need an alarm clock to wake me up. I just hear a knock at the door of my heart, and this automatically awakens me. Then, I hear the Lord say, "Cho, it's our time! I desire to fellowship with you now." Yet, this abiding relationship with Christ did not come by simply asking.

What do we seek?

We are to seek the Lord, for in Him are hidden all things that are precious: "In whom are hid all the treasures of wisdom and knowledge" (Col. 2:3).

In Colossians Paul pictures the church as a treasure field. In the field is hidden great treasure. Yet, the treasure is not material, it is spiritual: wisdom and knowledge.

When young Christians pray, they normally approach the

throne of God in time of need. Therefore, they go to God wanting something. This is both good and important. God wants us to ask. Yet, many view Christ simply as a grocery store to which they can bring their shopping list and have all the items on it filled. However, all of the great mysteries, the treasures of understanding, the source of total and complete joy, the essence of love, are waiting as hidden treasure in Christ. Those who are wise will sell all and buy the field so they may gain the treasure.

Moses said, "The secret things belong unto the Lord our God: but those things which are revealed belong unto us and to our children for ever" (Deut. 29:29). There is that which everyone can see in Scripture; but God wants to bring us into such close communion with Himself that He may share His most intimate treasures of wisdom and understanding. Treasure would not be treasure if it were easily accessible. Therefore, God's spiritual treasure must be sought in prayer.

I learned many years ago that it takes effort to get the treasures that God desires to give me: "I love them that love me; and those that seek me early shall find me. Riches and honor are with me; yea, durable riches and righteousness. My fruit is better than gold, yea, than fine gold; and my revenue than choice silver" (Prov. 8:17–19).

The lazy Christian is not willing to seek. He never enters into the fullness of the blessing which God has desired him to enter. It takes discipline and effort to live your life at the doorpost of the Lord. Remember, I am now pastoring the largest church in the world with over 370,000 members. I am extremely busy. Why do so many people come to my church? Is it only the cell system? Although the cell system has been the most effective means by which most of our members have come to Christ, this is not the main reason thousands wait seven times on Sunday to get a seat in each one of our services. They come to be fed the meat of the Word of God. Where do I receive my messages? I get them from my Lord in prayer and intimate communion and fellowship. This is imperative for all wise Christians: "Hear instruction, and be wise, and refuse it not   Blessed is the man that heareth me, watching daily at my gates, waiting at the posts of my doors. For whoso findeth me findeth life, and shall obtain (or bring forth) favor of the Lord" (Prov. 8:33–35).

If your Christian life is not exciting, you have not learned to seek the Lord. If your study of the Word of God does not bring fresh insight into spiritual reality, then you may have never entered the second phase of prayer: seek and ye shall find!

6

Prayer Is Intercession

A

Although prayer is petitioning God; although it is also seeking Him in deep fellowship and communion; it is also interceding before Him in the Holy Spirit. So the prayer of intercession is the third level of prayer in which we share the burden of Christ for a person, circumstance or need anywhere in the world. Intercession is the level of prayer where we may become a partaker of Christ's suffering.

When I pray in the Holy Spirit, I know that some of my prayers are for people and circumstances in other parts of the world. I may not know the exact need, but the Holy Spirit does—and He uses me to pray through until I know that God has met that need.

A missionary friend told me a miraculous story which indicates the importance of intercession. A missionary team was in a desert in Africa. They were hampered in their travel because of a wind storm that forced them off their path. In two days their water supply had run out. They wandered helplessly in the desert, suffering from dehydration. Suddenly there appeared a pool of water and they were saved. Upon returning to the place of their deliverance, they saw that the pool did not exist. At the time of their greatest need, someone was interceding in prayer and God performed a miracle.

In 1964, I met a lady who shared with me her experience of interceding for our church. After founding my first church outside Seoul, I pioneered a church in the downtown area of our nation's capital. Twenty years before I started the church in Seoul, the lady saw three visions of the church. After each vision, she would intercede for us in the Holy Spirit. When she was praying in 1944, we were still under Japanese occupation and there was no thought of our church. Yet, the Holy Spirit knew that this church, called the Sudaemoon Church because of the area in which it was located, would become the Full Gospel Central Church.

God used this faithful woman of intercessional prayer to cause the Holy Spirit to brood over that area, years before the vision came to pass. Just as the seed brings forth life in the human plane of existence, so also the Holy Spirit carries within Him all of the dynamics of life when He broods over an area.

This point is so important that I must elaborate on it further. When a child is conceived, the woman's egg and the man's sperm have an intricate code which is the actual blueprint of the future as determined within this genetic code. As the Holy Spirit brings forth life, so also much of the dynamics of the life is determined by the will of God implemented by the Holy Spirit.

In 1944, no one in downtown Seoul ever imagined that in the future, in that very area, God would raise up the means by which the whole nation of Korea would be affected by the gospel. Yet, the Holy Spirit, knowing the mind of God, knew; therefore, He raised up a faithful "prayer-warrior" who would intercede in the Holy Spirit twenty years before the reality of that intercession ever became obvious.

The lady actually saw the church as the largest church in the world. She was like Simeon and Anna (read Luke 2:25–39). Both Simeon and Anna knew that the child before them, who was only eight days old, would be the Messiah of Israel.

What are the qualities of an intercessor?

Simeon is a perfect example of the qualities an intercessor should possess:

1. He was devout! A person who enters the ministry of intercession should be given to prayer.
2. He was patient! The Scripture says that Simeon waited for the Consolation of Israel. While most people were looking for a political solution, Simeon knew that Israel's solution was spiritual. Therefore, he could wait many years before seeing the results of his prayers.
3. He was full of the Holy Spirit! Only a man who has the Holy Spirit upon him can carry the weight of intercessional prayer.
4. He trusted! It had been revealed to Simeon that he would see the results of his prayer before death. Therefore, he went faithfully to the temple daily for many years until the day came when Christ was brought to the temple.
5. He was a man of vision! Simeon's prophecy over the Christ child brought marvel to Joseph and Mary. Therefore, he saw more about Christ than His natural mother and step-father.

Before Christ's birth, the Holy Spirit had raised up two faithful intercessors. They spent many years fasting and praying for the coming of the Messiah. God caused them to live long enough to see what they had prayed for. Therefore, their ministry of intercessional prayer has forever been recorded in Scripture.

Intercessional prayer is necessary in the fulfillment of God's divine will. This does not mean that God is incapable of bringing His will to pass, but He has chosen to include us in the realization of His will. Therefore, those who enter a ministry of intercession actually become an integral part of the fulfillment of God's plans and purposes.

Why is intercession necessary?

Before we understand the necessity of intercession, we must see what we, as followers of Christ, are in this earth.

We are the salt of the earth (see Matt. 5:13)!

Salt gives flavor to what it comes in contact with. Job said, "Can that which is unsavory be eaten without salt?" (Job 6:6). The church is to function on this earth as salt. Our presence on earth causes God not to destroy this sinful earth, as He did Sodom and Gomorrah. God places on us the responsibility for withholding final judgment, giving man the time to either accept or reject Jesus Christ as Savior.

Similarly, we are ambassadors for Christ (2 Cor. 5:20). We therefore have been sent in an official capacity by our natural government (the kingdom of God) to represent its interests on foreign soil. The normal practice of governments at war is to first withdraw their ambassadors. Therefore, our remaining on this earth means that God is still forbearing this world's sin and there is still time to preach the Gospel.

Salt also restrains the process of corruption. Before the days of refrigeration, travelers had to cover their meat with salt to insure that it would not spoil. The spirit of antichrist has been at work since the first century. John wrote, "And every spirit that confesseth not that Jesus Christ is come in the flesh is not of God: and this is that spirit of antichrist, whereof ye have heard that it should come; and even now already is it in the world. Ye are of God, little children, and have overcome them: because greater is He that is in you, than he that is in the world" (1 John 4:3–4).

The spirit of antichrist, which is the spirit of lawlessness, has been at work with increasing influence in the world. Eventually, this spirit will produce the actual antichrist. The Holy Spirit, through the church, is holding back these anti-God forces, until this positive force is removed.

As we mature as Christians, we realize that being a Christian not only brings privilege, but also responsibility. As the main barrier to Satan's influence in this world, we must see the importance of intercessional prayer.

If we don't catch the vision of our role as the salt of this earth and lazily allow evil to gain control of the natural circumstances which prevail in our respective countries, then the salt would have lost its savor. At that time, Jesus said, "It is thenceforth good for nothing, but to be cast out, and to be trodden under foot of men" (Matt. 5:13).

We have also been called by God as a kingdom of priests. As a kingly priesthood, we have been given authority. The job of the Old Testament priest was to intercede for his people before the Mercy Seat of God. So also, in our prayers of intercession, we function in our role as New Testament priests standing in the gap for the needs of God's people.

God has determined that He will bring His children into co-rulership with Jesus Christ. He does not rule over us, not giving us any responsibility; but He has delegated His authority to us to assist in His dominion over this earth. "And hath put all things under his feet, and gave him to be head over all things to the church, which is his body, the fullness of him that filleth all in all" (Eph. 1:22–23). In Ephesians 2, Paul amplifies our role as rulers, "and hath raised us up together, and made us sit together in heavenly places in Christ Jesus" (v. 6).

In our exercise of spiritual authority, we are the recipients of both our natural knowledge and wisdom, which has been quickened by the Holy Spirit. We also have spiritual knowledge which far surpasses our natural knowledge. This knowledge is given to us by the Holy Spirit (see 1 Cor. 2:7–10).

The most quoted Old Testament passage in the New Testament is Psalm 110. To better understand how our authority can be used in intercessional prayer, it is important for us to study this Psalm carefully.

I quote Psalm 110 from the New King James Version of the Bible:

> The LORD said to my Lord,
> "Sit at My right hand,

> Till I make Your enemies Your
>   footstool."
> 2 The Lord shall send the rod of Your
>   strength out of Zion.
> Rule in the midst of Your enemies!
>
> 3 Your people *shall be* volunteers
>   In the day of Your power;
>   In the beauties of holiness,
>   from the womb of the morning,
>   You have the dew of Your youth.
> 4 The Lord has sworn
>   And will not relent,
>   "You *are* a priest forever
>   According to the order of
>   Melchizedek."
>
> 5 The Lord *is* at Your right hand;
>   He shall execute kings in the day of
>   His wrath.
> 6 He shall judge among the nations,
>   He shall fill *the places* with dead
>   bodies,
>   He shall execute the heads of many
>   countries.
> 7 He shall drink of the brook by the
>   wayside;
>   Therefore He shall lift up the head.

In this important Psalm, Christ is pictured as both the supreme ruler of the earth and a high priest according to the spiritual order of Melchizedek. Hebrews amplifies Christ's role as a spiritual priest: ". . . seeing he ever liveth to make intercession . . ." (Heb. 7:25). Christ's rulership is unique in that He rules in the middle of His enemies. David as king in the middle of his enemies had a physical throne. So Christ is in complete control without the obvious possession of the physical thrones of power in this earth.

The rod, which in Scripture is the sign of authority, comes out of Zion: the name used for God's people. Therefore, the way that the world experiences the dominion of Christ on this present world is through the exercising of the church's authority, particularly in intercession.

Now that we have understanding of our spiritual place on this earth as salt, kingly priests and sharers in Christ's throne, we are able to see how intercession works and why it is necessary.

As we saw in Daniel's prayer, Satan opposes the will of God—not only as it relates to the church, but as it relates to the entire world. Having been given authority over this age (Satan is called the god of this age), all of his might is directed against God's people, who, we have seen, are called to exercise Christ's authority.

Knowing that the church is the main obstacle to his purposes on earth, Satan is out to devour us as a roaring lion. Yet, the gospel of Christ must be preached and nations must be brought to the knowledge of God. These are two conflicting interests. And as we have learned through history, wars are fought because of conflicting interests among nations.

In intercession, the Christian enters into the priestly function of providing an earthly base for God's heavenly interests. This age has become the battleground between the two opposing forces, but God has a group in the foreign land that is able to bring the influence of the age to come into this age. Therefore, this natural world can be brought under the obvious control of the kingdom of God.

Moses lifted up his hands as Israel warred with or against her enemies; yet, when Moses allowed his hands to fall, Israel suffered. This is a clear symbol of intercession at work.

The cost of intercession

Before we can understand the cost of intercessional prayer, we must understand Christ's present suffering. When Saul was on the road to Damascus, he suddenly saw a blinding light. While his companions heard thunder, Saul heard a clear voice from heaven, "Saul, Saul, why persecutest thou me?"

Paul's response was: "Who art thou, Lord?"

Christ answered: "I am Jesus who thou persecutest."

Saul, later called the apostle Paul, never thought he was persecuting the Lord Jesus Christ. He was only persecuting the church. Yet, the Lord did not ask him why he persecuted His people—He asked why Paul persecuted Him.

We are the Body of Christ. Whatever we as His members feel, He as the head of the Body feels. Pain and suffering are never felt on the surface of our wound, but actual pain is felt in the brain, located in the head. The brain is able to project the pain to the part of the body that is being hurt so that that part can make a proper adjustment. So it is with the Body of Christ. What we feel, He feels; what we suffer, He suffers; yet, as the Head, His suffering is more intense.

It is true that those who have the potential to hurt us most are those closest to us. Unfortunately, some Christians go back to the world, having rejected the precious Lord who saved them. In Hebrews it says: "Seeing they crucify to themselves the Son of God afresh, and put him to an open shame" (Heb. 6:6). Therefore, Christ suffers the pain suffered at the cross each time a Christian turns back to the world.

In intercessional prayer, the Christian shares the suffering of Christ over a particular need in His Body. In Africa, a minister was preaching in a large crusade. During the night, he woke up in tears. As he began to pray, he heard himself saying a strange name, over and over again. The pain he suffered was intense as he continued his prayer. After several hours the burden lifted, and the intercession was complete. The next day the newspapers told a strange story. During the night, a Christian village had been massacred. The name of the village was the same name that the minister had been weeping over the night before. Christ suffered the pain of His people; but He was able to find someone willing to share in His suffering and intercede in the spirit.

Paul said: "That I may know him, and the power of his resurrection, and the fellowship of his suffering" (Phil. 3:10). In this scripture, Paul showed that he was not only willing to enjoy the resurrection power of Christ; but he was willing to fellowship with Christ in His suffering.

In our church, we have committed ourselves to enter a ministry of intercession. We have learned petition in prayer, so we are seeing our needs met. We are committed to devotional prayer, so we are enjoying fellowship with our precious Lord. Yet, we are more than ever committed to the prayer of intercession; therefore we are seeing revival in our country and will see it in the whole world.

No other place on earth has three to ten thousand people fasting and praying continuously. We are serious about the battle God has commanded us to fight. We are serious about the spiritual weapons that will insure our victory. We are conscious of the battlefield, the hearts of men throughout the world. And we are convinced of the final victory we can share with the King of Glory.

What door do we enter in prayers of intercession?

Besides its common use as an entrance to a house or building, a door is used metaphorically as the entrance into any spiritual experience or the entrance to opportunity. Therefore, Jesus said, "I am the door." Christ is the means by which man can reach the Father. Paul used the word as an entrance to opportunity.

Paul said, "Furthermore, when I came to Troas to preach Christ's gospel, and a door was opened unto me of the Lord, I had no rest in my spirit . . ." (2 Cor. 2:12–13).

John, when writing to the church at Philadelphia, shares this revelation from Christ, "I know thy works: behold, I have set before thee an open door, and no man can shut it . . ." (Rev. 3:8).

Not only is a door a place of opportunity to preach the gospel of Jesus Christ to a community; it is also an opportunity for an individual, as the Lord confirms: "Behold, I stand at the door, and knock: if any man hear my voice, and open the door, I will come in to him, and will sup with him, and he with me" (Rev. 3:20).

There are doors to nations and ethnic groups that can be

opened. Once the door is opened, they are able to receive faith and believe: "And when they were come, and had gathered the church together, they rehearsed all that God had done with them, and how he had opened the door of faith unto the Gentiles" (Acts 14:27).

Going through a door of opportunity means that we face spiritual opposition from the principalities and powers that keep nations from hearing and responding to the gospel: "For a great door and effectual is opened unto me, and there are many adversaries" (2 Cor. 16:9).

Only the Lord Jesus Christ can open a door that has been shut to the gospel: "Furthermore, when I came to Troas to preach Christ's gospel, and a door was opened unto me of the Lord" (2 Cor. 2:12).

How do we get the doors of faith and opportunity opened? We have seen that Christ must open the door. However, God has made us members of His body. That means that the Head has chosen to function through His body on earth. So it takes prayers of intercession to stand against the spiritual forces keeping the doors shut. Once the prayers break through, Christ can open the door and an entire city, nation or race can be saved. Paul confirms this: "Withal praying also for us, that God would open unto us a door of utterance, to speak the mystery of Christ, for which I am also in bonds: That I may make it manifest, as I ought to speak" (Col. 4:3–4).

Not only does Christ desire to open doors of opportunity to His people, so they may preach the gospel; but, doors of revelation and understanding must also be opened. Jesus continually repeats the phrase: "he that has ears, let him hear!" This statement made to the churches in Revelation in chapters 2 and 3 indicates that we often don't understand what we are hearing. The door of understanding must be opened for our minds to comprehend what God desires to reveal to us: "After this I looked, and, behold, a door was opened in heaven: and the first voice which I heard was as it were of a trumpet talking with me; which said, 'Come up hither, and I will show thee things which must be hereafter. And immediately I was in the spirit . . .'" (Rev. 4:1–2).

In Acts we see how God can open a door of opportunity and keep the door open so we may preach the gospel without spiritual hindrance. Paul had been accused and had been brought to Rome, a city which was at that time the center of sin. Paul prayed and asked others to intercede for him. Finally, the door to Rome was opened: "And Paul dwelt two whole years in his own hired house, and received all that came in unto him. Preaching the kingdom of God, and teaching those things which concern the Lord Jesus Christ, with all confidence, no man forbidding him" (Acts 28:30–31). So, the Book of Acts ends. It is important that the Holy Spirit closes the Book of Acts with a door open. Of course, most of us know that Acts ends without the proper grammatical ending. We can ascertain from this grammatical flaw (Luke, being a doctor, had an excellent command of Greek) that the Book of Acts is still being written as the church still is performing the "acts" of the Holy Spirit.

Although we know that Paul was finally executed, the official history of the early church ends on a positive note. No man can forbid the preaching of the gospel once God opens the door of spiritual opportunity!

God can even block the opposition that comes from our own brothers and sisters in Christ. It is an unfortunate fact that so much of our energy is wasted because of the lack of unity in the church. Instead of fighting our real enemy the devil, so many of God's people fight each other. However, an open spiritual door can also block the opposition that comes from within. Paul also experienced this in Acts 28, "And they said unto him. 'We neither received letters out of Judea (the center of Paul's opposition) concerning thee, neither any of the brethren that came showed or spake any harm of thee'" (v. 21).

Therefore, it is obvious that what is needed throughout the whole world is for Christians to understand and enter into the third level of prayer: intercession.

Knock, and the door shall be opened!

As I stated before, we cannot be too distinctive in our dividing the three types of prayer. One can petition, commune and intercede in the same prayer time. It is hard to intercede without communion with Christ. Our petitions will be more effective by communion. Our intercession includes petitions, fellowship and communion. However, by understanding the three types of prayer, we can pray more effectively.

As new Christians, we approach prayer as the means by which we can receive from God. In time, we begin to mature and desire more. The newness of our experience is no longer as strong, so we may think we are slipping. What is actually happening is that we are being weaned spiritually from our infant formula and are being prepared for adult food. Then, we must enter into spiritual communion and fellowship with Christ, through the work of the Holy Spirit.

Once we have begun our personal relationship with Christ, we begin to feel what He feels. We can no longer allow things to continue as they are and we volunteer in the army of prayer. David prophesied, "Your people shall be volunteers in the day of Your power."

Why are we experiencing continuous revival in Korea? We have volunteered to pray until the gospel is preached in the whole world. The doors will be opened as the spiritual forces are bound in the name of Jesus!

Part III

The Forms of Prayer

Introduction

△

Prayer takes on different forms in our Christian lives. It is my desire to share with you the forms of prayer that we practice at the Yoido Full Gospel Church in Seoul, Korea. Not that we have exhausted all forms of prayer. Perhaps you may know a form of prayer that I have not included in this section. However, what I am about to share with you is based on our experience and in many ways explains the source of our unique church growth.

7

Your Personal Devotional Life

△

To guarantee our continual personal growth as a Christian, we must have a regular personal devotional life. If we stop praying, we begin to slow down as we move from impetus to momentum, as we have explained previously.

In many parts of the world, Christianity has become a traditional religion—full of ritualism and with little pulsating life. In today's fast-moving age, people find it difficult to institute and maintain a personal devotional life. Television plays an increasingly dominant role in our daily lives. This wastes even more important time that can be devoted to prayer. What is happening is that the more advanced the civilization, the more distractions exist to keep men and women from praying every day. The only way to keep from falling into this trap is to see the extreme importance of daily devotions.

There are many reasons we should pray daily. The following are just two of them:

1. Our day must begin in prayer for then, God responds. God loves to move in our hearts early: "There is a river, the streams whereof shall make glad the city of God, the holy place of the tabernacles of the Most High. God is in the midst of her; she shall

not be moved: God shall help her, and that right early (Hebrew—during the dawn)" (Psa. 46:4–5).

"Awake up, my glory; awake, psaltery and harp: I myself will awake early" (Psa. 57:8). This statement is repeated by David in Psalm 108, verse two. Both verses show David's practice of getting up early every morning to praise and worship the Lord. It is no wonder that God testified David was a man after His own heart.

However, David not only praised and worshiped God early in the morning, but he *sought* the Lord as well during this precious early time: "O God, thou art my God; early will I seek thee: my soul thirsteth for thee, my flesh longeth for thee in a dry and thirsty land, where no water is; to see thy power and thy glory, so as I have seen thee in the sanctuary. Because thy lovingkindness is better than life, my lips shall praise thee. Thus will I bless thee while I live: I will lift up my hands in thy name" (Psa. 63:1–4).

God has promised those who make it a practice to get up early to seek the Lord would find Him: "I love them that love me; and those that seek me early shall find me" (Prov. 8:17).

2. When we begin our day in prayer, we shall have the spiritual and physical strength to carry out our responsibilities: "With my soul have I desired thee in the night; yea, with my spirit within me will I seek thee early: for when thy judgments are in the earth, the inhabitants of the world will learn righteousness" (Isa. 26:9).

Isaiah learned the judgments of God in his spirit as he sought the Lord early in the morning. I have learned that the wisdom of God that comes to me in my early morning devotions allows me to be more effective. In a few minutes I know what God wants in each situation. I don't have to spend days judging a matter because I have the mind of Christ.

Our devotional time must not only include prayer, but it should also include personal Bible reading!

So often those of us in the pastoral ministry only look into the Scripture to get messages to preach. Yet, we must read the Bible to be spiritually nourished for our own hearts: "Thy word have I hid in mine heart, that I might not sin against thee" (Psa. 119:11). "The entrance of thy words giveth light; it giveth understanding unto the simple" (Psa. 119:130).

God can speak to us from the Scripture if we give Him the opportunity. The morning hours find our minds clear from all of the conflicts of the day; therefore, we are capable of receiving His direction and instruction that can come from His holy Word.

As a minister of the gospel, I must remember that my teaching and preaching must come as an overflow of my personal study. God's people who hear me will be blessed as I am blessed from the Word of God. I can only motivate if I am motivated. I can only inspire, as I am inspired by the Holy Spirit. Therefore, I must read the Bible as part of my daily devotional life.

8

Your Family Devotions

△

Although it is well known and often repeated, this is still true: Families who pray together stay together!

Not only in America, but in most of the world, television is increasingly becoming the center of most family activity. Between video games, news and network programming, families are finding it increasingly difficult to eat together, let alone pray together. Reports have been published showing that the average North American child spends forty hours a week watching television and each year, the time increases.

The divorce rate has skyrocketed. In some communities more people are getting divorced than are getting married! Satan seems to be winning the war which is being waged in the home. What will prevent the battle from affecting our homes? The answer is family devotions!

The family's devotional time should include singing, Bible reading and prayer. Honesty should be allowed during this time, especially for the children. As I shared with you what my oldest son said during one of our family devotions, so I allow all my children to express their feelings, fears and frustrations. This way we can keep open the flow of communication between us and we can be drawn closer in an honest relationship.

The alarming statistics which are now being published show that many suicides occur within the teenage demographical group. Young people feel the increasing pressures of alienation from their parents, plus coping with the strong conforming peer pressure. Therefore, many of our young people have turned to drugs, illicit sex and alcohol. Once these artificial stimulants no longer work, young people plunge into despair and take their own lives.

Psychologists say that the family is the only bastion of hope left for today's young people. By keeping honest communication with our children, they will be strong enough to resist the devil's attack. Satan also uses false religion to attack our young people. We are all familiar with religious cults that offer young men and women the pseudo-atmosphere of a home and family. Our strongest defense against this is a strong family devotional life.

As God has chosen to share His burden with us, we should also learn to share our prayer-burdens with our children. Why should our children see the results of our concerns and then be left out regarding the reason behind them? How will they know how to handle problems by turning them over to the Lord, if they don't see us do the same?

In our family, we usually gather in a prayer circle daily. We hold hands and begin to pray. One of my sons may be having a problem with one of his courses in school. This problem immediately becomes the problem of the entire family and must be brought before the throne of grace in prayer. For example, my prayer will be, "Dear Lord, please help my oldest son with this test he is about to have. Let him learn his subject so well that he may get a high grade for Your glory. Amen!"

My wife has concerns which are important too. My wife, Grace, is a most important part of my ministry. Yet, her concerns may be for the publishing company she runs; or the music program she is involved with; or, even for the new dress she may need for a special function. Her concerns are the concerns of us all. This brings our family into a oneness that cannot be easily broken

9

Prayer in the Church Service

△

One of the most important ministries of the Full Gospel Central Church is the prayer in unison we have during every service. We always open our services with everyone present praying together at the same time. We may pray for the salvation and protection of our nation. Having been oppressed by the Japanese for many years, and suffering invasion from the Communist North Koreans; realizing that freedom, especially religious freedom, is so precious that it must be protected; we pray earnestly for our country.

We also pray for our leaders together. God has commanded us to do this and if we don't obey Him, we will get the government we deserve. Therefore, we pray for our president, as well as our other leaders. For this reason, I have complete liberty to preach the gospel in my church, on television, and on radio. Many, especially in Europe, don't have the freedom to preach over the public airwaves. In Korea, we appreciate this freedom and guard it through prayer.

We pray in unison for the thousands of requests that come to us from America, Japan and the rest of the world. Every service finds me standing next to our "prayer request podium," placing my hands on the requests and all of us praying together. Before the requests are sent to Prayer Mountain, hundreds of thousands of people pray earnestly over them in each one of our seven services.

We especially pray for a world-wide revival that will allow every nation to hear the gospel, fulfilling our mission till Christ returns. As the largest church in the world, we recognize that we have been given a special responsibility to pray for the church of Jesus Christ in every nation.

After my message, we again pray together. This time we ask that the Holy Spirit will take the Word and apply it to our hearts so we can be doers of the Word and not hearers only.

When we pray together, we pray with determination and assurance. When I hear my people praying, it sounds like the forceful roar of a mighty waterfall. We know God must hear the sincerity of our prayer because we are praying in unison and unity!

As we pray together, the power of God is manifested in our midst. Many have been healed, delivered and filled with the Holy Spirit as we have united in prayer. If one can put a thousand to flight and two can handle ten thousand, can you imagine hundreds of thousands united in prayer—the power is beyond comprehension!

"O magnify the Lord with me, and let us exalt his name together" (Psa. 34:3).

10

Prayer in the Cell Meeting

A

The cell system is the very basis of our church. I discovered this concept during one of the most difficult hours in my ministry. As a pastor of a church with three thousand members, I felt that I could do everything, and I tried to. I would preach, visit and pray for the sick; yet, as my church grew, I became weaker. One Sunday, as I interpreted for an American evangelist, I collapsed. Believing that what I needed was more dedication and fortitude, I tried again, but I failed to finish the service. I was rushed to the Red Cross hospital.

"Pastor Cho, you may be able to live, but you must give up the ministry!" With these discomfiting words, my doctor greeted me in the hospital after I regained consciousness.

"What could I do except preach the gospel?" I whispered to myself quietly. The realization of what had just been said fell on me like a heavy boulder.

I have discovered that God sometimes has to go to unusual extremes to get my attention. I must admit, He got my attention in the hospital! The days that followed were times of reappraisal for my life. Yet, during that dark hour, I discovered the basic ingredient to the unlimited potential for growth in my church: the cell system.

Luke records a similar incident in Acts 6. When the number of the disciples was still small, the twelve apostles were able to do all of the administrative work in the church. However, if this situation had remained the same, the church would have never been able to grow beyond the number that was in Jerusalem. The way God changed the thinking of the apostles was to allow them to meet the potentially devastating problem which is described in the sixth chapter.

The ethnic division which almost caused the first split had to be solved. What resulted was that the apostles realized they could not carry on the entire work of the ministry by themselves. Therefore, they called seven men and appointed them as deacons. The deacons took care of the administration of the church and the apostles gave themselves to their original calling: "But we will give ourselves continually to prayer, and to the ministry of the Word" (Acts 6:4).

The problem seen in this chapter caused God's men to review their situation and receive the wisdom of the Holy Spirit. That wisdom would cause them to delegate their authority to others, thereby allowing for unlimited growth.

I noticed that in several places in Acts, the disciples met in large and small groups. The following are some quotes from Acts and Romans which opened my eyes to the validity of the cell system:

"And they, continuing daily with one accord in the temple, and breaking bread from house to house, did eat their meat with gladness and singleness of heart, praising God, and having favor with all the people. And the Lord added to the church daily such as should be saved" (Acts 2:46–47).

"And daily in the temple, and in every house, they ceased not to teach and preach Jesus Christ" (Acts 5:42).

"And how I kept back nothing that was profitable unto you, but have showed you, and have taught you publicly, and from house to house" (Acts 20:20).

"Likewise greet the church that is in their house" (Rom. 16:5).

These and other Scriptures gave me the direction I needed. Since then, our cell system has grown to the point that at this time we have over twenty thousand cells in our church. If each one of those cells just leads two families to Christ in one year, that gives us forty thousand new families. Since the normal family consists of four members, that gives us a yearly growth rate of one hundred and sixty thousand new converts. This does not count the members who are led to Christ through television, radio and our Sunday worship services. Therefore, the continual growth of our church depends mainly on our cell system.

Our cell meetings consist of five to ten families. They may meet in homes, which may be convenient for evening meetings or daytime women's meetings; schools, which is best for our student cells; factories, for our workers' cell meetings; or, they may meet in a room of a restaurant, which is good for businessmen's meetings. Wherever they meet, they are the church in action. Our large church building is the place where the people come together to share the Word of God and enjoy the worship of our church combined; yet our church is really meeting in thousands of locations everywhere in our area.

In our cell meetings, the members pray for each other's needs. The cell leader visits them when they get sick and prays for their healing. Our people have been taught the central nature of prayer, so they pray over everything. They fervently pray for the church, the nation and for a continuation of revival in Korea and throughout the world. They also pray for potential new converts so the church may continue to grow.

In our cell leaders conferences, I stress that the cells must have a clear goal in their prayers; therefore, our cells paint a clear picture of their goal as they pray in faith. Since it is much easier to lead a person you know to Jesus Christ, the cell member witnesses to his neighbor, friend or relative. When God opens the door for this potential convert to be saved, the member will share this with the rest of the cell and they will not stop praying until that person comes to Christ.

We have learned that we are at war against Satan in this earth. Our opposition is the devil and his demonic spirits. Our battlefield is the hearts of all men and women. Our goal is that all may come to know the saving grace of our Lord and Savior, Jesus Christ. Therefore, we plan carefully: we have a strategy, we have a plan, and we execute that plan like a well-trained army. Yet, most importantly, we bathe our plans in prayer so that God may breathe His breath of life into our efforts and they will be fruitful.

I have not followed a secret formula in the mighty church growth we are experiencing. What I have done is simply take the Word of God seriously. There is no question in my mind that what has been done in Korea can also be duplicated in every part of the world. The key is prayer!

11

Prayer at Prayer Mountain

A

What we have called Prayer Mountain is really much more than a retreat area dedicated to prayer. Originally, this land was purchased for a church cemetery. Since Korea has been a traditionally Buddhist country, having a church burial place was very important to us.

When our present church was being built in 1973, the dollar was devalued. This caused the Korean won (which is tied in value to the American dollar) to suffer, and we entered into a deep recession. Then, the oil crisis hit us, worsening our already fragile economy. Our people lost their jobs and our income went down.

Having signed contracts with the construction company, and experiencing an unprecedented increase in building costs, I suffered greatly, seeing the possibility of a financial collapse. Despondently, I sat in my unfinished church building, wishing the still bare rafters would just fall on me.

During this crucial time in my ministry, a group from our church went to the property and started building a place to pray, mainly for their suffering pastor. Although I saw the need for this in our church, my concern was the added expenses that kept piling up on my desk.

Seeing that only a miraculous intervention of God would deliver us from a catastrophe, I joined the intercessors at Prayer Mountain. One evening, while we were meeting to pray on the ground floor of our unfinished church, several hundred joined me in prayer. An old woman walked slowly in my direction. As she approached the platform, I noticed that tears were filling her eyes. She bowed and said, "Pastor, I want to give these items to you so that you may sell them for a few pennies to help with our building fund."

I looked down, and in her hands were an old rice bowl and a pair of chopsticks. Then, I said to her: "Sister, I can't take these necessities from you!"

"But Pastor, I am an old woman. I have nothing of value to give to my Lord; yet, Jesus has graciously saved me. These items are the only things in the world I possess!" she exclaimed, tears now flowing freely down her wrinkled cheeks. "You must let me give these to Jesus. I can place my rice on old newspapers and I can use my hands to feed myself. I know that I will die soon, so I don't want to meet Jesus without giving Him something on this earth." As she finished speaking, everyone there began to weep openly. The Holy Spirit's presence filled the place and we all began to pray in the Spirit.

A businessman in the back of the group was deeply moved and said, "Pastor Cho, I want to buy that rice bowl and chopsticks for one thousand dollars!" With that, everyone started to pledge their possessions. My wife and I sold our small home and gave the money to the church. This spirit of giving saved us from financial ruin.

As the years have gone by, Prayer Mountain has grown to be a place where thousands of people go daily to have their needs met, fasting and praying. We have added a modern ten-thousand-seat auditorium which is now too small to hold the crowds that come. Attendance varies, but normally at least three thousand people are daily praying, fasting, worshiping and praising our holy and precious Lord. In this atmosphere of concentrated prayer, healings and miracles are a common occurrence.

Last year, over 300,000 people registered at Prayer Mountain.

This makes this "haven of prayer" the front line of our attack on the devil's forces on this earth. Nowhere in this world are there more people praying and fasting. God hears our prayers and the answers are too numerous to mention.

In the next chapter on fasting and prayer, I will more fully discuss the method by which we practice this biblical means of getting needs met. However, I cannot emphasize enough the importance of fasting and prayer in order to see revival begin and continue.

Not only do we have group prayer at Prayer Mountain, but we also have individual prayer in our "prayer grottos." These small cubicles are actually cut into the side of a hill. At these prayer grottos, people can get very still and quiet before God. In my own "prayer closet," I can shut the door and commune with my Heavenly Father in concentrated and prolonged prayer.

Previously, I called Prayer Mountain a "haven of prayer." The reason I did this is that preparations are being made that will house thousands of people not only from Korea, but also from every corner of the earth. I believe there are many Christians who are longing for a place where they can meet God in a dynamic way. Not that God can't be found everywhere men seek Him in spirit and in truth; but, there is no place on earth that has more concentrated prayer than Prayer Mountain. Christians are not satisfied with just hearing about the moving of God; they desire to see what God is doing. Therefore, roads are being built, proper housing is being erected and facilities are being enlarged to accommodate what God is about to do.

David wrote, "He turneth the wilderness into a standing water, and dry ground into watersprings; And there he maketh the hungry to dwell, that they may prepare a city for habitation" (Psa. 107:35–36).

And again, "So the heathen shall fear the name of the Lord, and all the kings of the earth thy glory. When the Lord shall build up Zion, he shall appear in his glory. He will regard the prayer of the destitute, and not despise their prayer. This shall be written for the generation to come: and the people which shall be created shall praise the Lord" (Psa. 102:15–18).

12

All-Night Prayer Meetings

A

How can thousands of people spend every Friday night in prayer? Many people have asked me this question all over the world. If people can spend all night at a disco, why can't dedicated Christians spend all night praying and worshiping the Lord? It all depends on what and where our priorities are. Either we are going to be serious about revival or not!

Our people gather at 10:30 at night and begin to pray quietly every Friday. I then give a strong teaching from the Word of God. Since I am not under the time pressure that I must live under on Sunday, I can take my time and teach for two hours. It should become obvious that we do follow a prescribed program. People would not come so faithfully if they just had to sit and pray the entire night.

Following our Bible study, we begin to pray. We pray for specific needs and problems in our church, as well as our own needs. After prayer, we begin to sing gospel songs. After the song service, one of my associate pastors will preach. Then, we sing again and get ready to hear personal testimonies of what God has done in our members' lives. There are so many miracles of God's grace taking place every week that there is no way possible to fit in all those who wish to testify. These mighty stories of God's provision cause us to want to sing again. Before we realize it, it is 4:30 A.M. and it's time to get ready for the Saturday early morning prayer meeting. After prayer, we are dismissed and go home rejoicing.

David was accustomed to spending all night in prayer. In Psalm 63, he calls his all-night prayer meetings "night watches" (see Psa. 63:6; 119:148).

Isaiah prophesied, "Ye shall have a song as in the night when a holy solemnity is kept; and gladness of heart, as when one goeth with a pipe to come into the mountain of the Lord, to the Mighty One of Israel" (30:29).

When the disciples were in prison, they did not spend the night complaining; they spent the night singing and praying. Therefore, God heard them and sent deliverance in the form of an angel.

The presence of the Lord is most important. Jesus promised us that when we gathered in His name, He would be there. It is easy to spend the night, when the sweet aroma of our Lord's presence fills the place where we are gathering.

In many parts of the world, Saturday is a day off for workers; but, in Korea, it is a normal working day. So people spending all Friday night in prayer means that, for many, they will go home and get ready to go to work. However, David stated that he could not give God what cost him nothing. Although it is not easy to spend the night in prayer, it has been the means by which we have been able to maintain the revival.

13

Fasting and Prayer

A

Fasting is voluntary and deliberate abstinence from food for the purpose of concentrated prayer. Usually, just food is abstained from, but on rare occasions and for short periods of time, water is abstained from as well.

In Christ's Sermon on the Mount, He taught His disciples about fasting. The teaching which our Lord gave also dealt with the motives of fasting: We should never fast to impress others. However, He expected His disciples to fast. He said, "When ye fast . . ." not "If ye fast."

Jesus was the example in fasting: "And Jesus being full of the Holy Ghost returned from Jordan, and was led by the Spirit into the wilderness, being forty days tempted of the devil. And in those days he did eat nothing: and when they were ended, he afterward hungered" (Luke 4:1-2).

After Christ's fast, Luke recorded: "And Jesus returned in the power of the Spirit . . ." (v. 14).

From the Scripture just quoted, we can deduce this: being full of the Holy Spirit does not necessarily cause one to walk in the power of the Spirit! I believe the way into power, especially in prayer, is to fast and pray.

Paul's ministry also began with fasting and prayer (see (Acts 9:9). Paul testified to the Corinthian church that he proved his ministry by his spiritual discipline: "in watchings, in fastings" (2 Cor. 6:5). Therefore, Paul was accustomed to fasting and praying—"watchings" meaning spending the night in prayer.

In public gatherings, the early church fasted and prayed in order to know the will of God. In Acts 13, the Holy Spirit was able to clearly direct the church: "Now there were in the church that was at Antioch certain prophets and teachers; as Barnabas, and Simeon that was called Niger, and Lucius of Cyrene, and Manaen, which had been brought up with Herod the tetrarch, and Saul. As these ministered to the Lord, and fasted, the Holy Ghost said, 'Separate me Barnabas and Saul for the work whereunto I have called them.' And when they had fasted and prayed . . . they sent them away" (Acts 13:1-3).

As the two apostles, Barnabas and Paul, started new churches, they taught the believers the same practice of fasting and praying that they had experienced in Antioch:

"And when they had preached the gospel to that city, and had taught many, they returned again to Lystra, and to Iconium, and Antioch. Confirming the souls of the disciples, and exhorting them to continue in the faith, and that we must through much tribulation enter into the kingdom of God. And when they had ordained them elders in every church, and had prayed with fasting, they commended them to the Lord, on whom they believed" (Acts 14:21-23).

The previous verse shows that prayer and fasting were a vital part of gaining direction from the Holy Spirit before ordaining church leadership. Fasting combined with prayer caused the early church to have clarity of mind and spirit to establish its foundations.

Fasting combined with prayer not only brings clarity of mind and spirit, releasing the voice of the Holy Spirit to give direction. It is also important for gaining spiritual and material victories. We see a perfect example of this in the Old Testament.

Jehoshaphat, the king of Judah, had received a report that

there was a large army massing to attack. The army that was amassing at Judah's borders came from Moab and Ammon. We in South Korea know the feeling of having a hostile army amassed at our border. Rather than trying to fight with armaments he did not have, the king used his spiritual resources: He proclaimed a national fast. Everyone gathered together, men and women, boys and girls; they all fasted and sought the Lord's intervention. The result of this national prayer and fasting was that God won a glorious victory. God gave the king directions on how to fight the enemy. I'm sure that no other battle had ever been fought like this one. Jehoshaphat appointed singers to praise the Lord before the army. When the enemy saw this, confusion came into their camp and they began to fight each other. It took three days for the spoils of the battle to be picked up, as God had given them victory without resorting to physical weapons (see 2 Chronicles 20:1–30).

When we begin to fast, we should get the proper mental attitude. We should not see the fast as a punishment, even though our bodies may rebel at first. Fasting should be viewed as a precious opportunity to get closer to our Lord, not distracted by the daily concern of eating. We should also see the fast as a means by which our prayers may be more perfectly focused. This will cause God to hear and move in our behalf. Fasting, when it is viewed in this way, will be much easier.

Normally I teach my people to begin to fast three days. Once they have become accustomed to three-day fasts, they will be able to fast for a period of seven days; then, they will move to ten-day fasts. Some have even gone for forty days, but this is not usually encouraged.

We have seen that fasting and prayer causes one to become much more spiritually sensitive to our Lord, causing more power in one's life to combat the forces of Satan. How does this work?

The desire for food is basic to all living creatures. It is one of the strongest motivational forces at work in the body, even before birth. Babies are born with the natural instinct to reach out for the mother's breast. If we can combine this intense natural desire with our natural spiritual desire for communion with our spiritual source, then what results is a much greater intensity: this is the purpose of prayer and fasting. By combining our natural and spiritual desires, we can cause the urgency of our petition to come up before the Throne of God with such intensity that He will hear and answer.

Desire is basic to prayer: "Delight thyself in the Lord and he shall give thee the desires of thine heart" (Psa. 37:40).

"Whatsoever ye desire, when ye pray believe that ye receive them, and ye shall have them" (Mark 11:24).

Therefore, the stronger the desire, the more effective the prayer!

In my experience, on the first day of fasting, there is no significant effect on the body. On the second day, hunger increases more dramatically. On the third and fourth days, the body begins to demand food and you feel the full physical effects of the abstinence. After the fifth and sixth days, the body adjusts to the new circumstance and you feel better. What is happening is that the body is now more efficient in breaking down the body fats that have been stored.

After the seventh day, the hunger pains disappear, although the body gets much weaker. However, there comes a clarity of thought and a freedom in prayer that is unusual.

God responds to sincerity

When we fast, God responds to our sincerity in willingly humbling ourselves. His mercy and grace are released by the voluntary humbling and afflicting of the soul in the individual, community and nation. As we see in many instances in the Old Testament, God fought for Israel when Israel humbled herself before Him.

Satan is always trying to get through to us as we succumb to our fleshly lusts. He cannot penetrate the blood of Christ, but we can give Him access through sin.

Paul calls Satan the prince of the power of the air, or the atmosphere around the earth. Jude's epistle says, "Likewise also these dreamers defile the flesh, reject authority, and speak evil of dignitaries. Yet Michael the archangel, when contending with the devil, when he disputed about the body of Moses, dared not bring against him a reviling accusation, but said, 'The Lord rebuke you!' But these speak evil of whatever they do not know; and whatever they know naturally, like brute beasts, in these things they corrupt themselves" (Jude 8–10, NKJV).

Both verses just quoted reveal something very significant about our adversary, the devil. Satan is a prince with considerable power. Jude also states that the devil cannot be treated lightly, as some Christians are accustomed to doing. Although his power has been destroyed over God's property, he is still a formidable opponent.

Jesus stated: ". . . the prince of this world cometh, and hath nothing in me." In other words, Satan had no landing field in Christ from which he could bring an attack against Him. We must also live our lives in such a way that the prince of this world has no ground that will accept his attack. Germany, before World War II, developed a network of loyal agents in many countries. Hitler knew that he would need loyal allies if his plan for world conquest would succeed. Hitler called this group of men and women the fifth column. We must see to it that we have no fifth column in us that is loyal to Satan.

How do we do this? Through prayer and fasting!

Through fasting and prayer, you can so concentrate the power of prayer on your own lusts: lust of the flesh, lust of the eyes and the pride of life; that you can live a holy and pure life in God's presence. Through prayer and fasting, the beachhead for Satan, which I have referred to as the fifth column, can be destroyed. Therefore, when the prince of this world comes, he can find no place in you.

The practical results of fasting and prayer will be a true and undefiled religion being lived out in your life: "Is not this the fast that I have chosen? to loose the bands of wickedness, to undo the heavy burdens, and to let the oppressed go free, and that ye break every yoke? Is it not to deal thy bread to the hungry, and that thou bring the poor that are cast out to thy house? when thou seest the naked, that thou cover him; and that thou hide not thyself from thine own flesh?" (Isa. 58:6–7). Fasting can break the bands of wickedness; it can cause the oppressed to go free; it can bring total and complete deliverance.

We are commanded to: ". . . undo the heavy burdens." When we see heavy burdens, in ourselves or in others, we can loose them through fasting and prayer. Whether these burdens be in health, business or family relationships, these burdens can be lifted.

Fasting and praying for others

As I have already stated, Prayer Mountain is dedicated to prayer and fasting; however, this prayer is not only for the needs of those present, but through concentrated prayer, we can see the thousands that write to our New York office prayed for as well. Once the prayer requests that arrive daily leave my desk and are prayed for by our congregation, they are sent to Prayer Mountain. An intercessor will pray and fast over the request, being already translated into Korean, until they witness in their heart that God has heard and the answer is on its way. By fasting, our praying intercessors have been sensitized to be keenly aware of the urgency of the request. They can therefore envision the need and visualize the answer. The testimonies that come to us of answered prayer are too many to include here. However, we have discovered that God hears and answers prayer and fasting combined.

People come from all over the world to pray and fast at Prayer Mountain and receive a miracle. A few years ago, a polio victim visited Prayer Mountain. She had heard of the miracles that took place at Prayer Mountain and was determined to come, not concerning herself with the physical difficulties involved in travel.

After sailing five days, she was met at the dock by one of our members who placed her on a train.

The young lady, only twenty-three years old, arrived with an expectancy that she would walk again. In the natural course of events, this seemed impossible: she had been severely crippled since she was three years old. But, through God, all things are possible! After checking in, she immediately started to build her faith by reading the Word of God, seeking all the promises of God.

As she was planning to stay three months, she determined to take two days out of every week to fast. During her stay, she was particularly impressed by the testimonies that she heard. Each time she heard someone testify to the miraculous power of God, her faith increased.

After the first month, there was no visual sign of healing: her legs were still mangled by the paralysis to which she had grown accustomed. During the second month, she felt renewed in her spirit and soul, but still unchanged in her body. However, during the third month, something began to happen! For the first time in many years, she could feel a sensation in her legs. Expecting a miracle, she cried out: "Help me stand up! Please, someone, help me stand on my feet! I know I am healed!"

Seeing the tears, and perceiving her excitement, a couple of our members joyously grabbed her arms and brought her to her feet. Yet, though her legs were feeling a sensation of blood rushing through her arteries and veins, she did not possess the strength to stand. Without showing any signs of disappointment, she slowly allowed herself to be seated again and continued praying. She knew that a creative miracle was necessary for the atrophied limbs to come back into use, so she patiently waited and continued to fast and pray.

After the three months were up, she left, still in a wheel-chair. But something had happened inside: she knew she was healed! Several months went by before I received a beautiful letter from this young woman. In her letter, she stated that it took persistence, but the miracle finally came. "Yes, Dr. Cho. Now I can walk!" she wrote me. "I still have a slight limp, but I am walking. I know that even the limp will disappear soon!" she stated in complete faith. This is only one of many miracles that have taken place at Prayer Mountain.

Will everyone be healed at Prayer Mountain if they fast and pray? Obviously, healing is not as simple as that. Some people get healed immediately, while others take longer. Yet, when people have great difficulty in getting healed, I have discovered that they may have unforgiveness in their hearts.

Forgiveness and healing

"If ye forgive men their trespasses, your heavenly Father will also forgive you: but if ye forgive not men their trespasses, neither will your father forgive your trespasses" (Matt. 6:14–15).

Many people have been wronged by their families, business associates and friends. They therefore seek justice, as they perceive justice to be. If justice is not rendered in their circumstances, they become hateful and bitter. Many of these people will develop physical symptoms that are directly attributable to their unforgiving attitude. They develop a root of bitterness that gives off poisons into their systems and suffer both mental and physical anguish.

"But I am right!" a lady told me once, after I shared with her what I have just shared with you. "My husband is guilty! I hate him!"

"Yes, sister," I replied. "But you are the one suffering from being crippled with arthritis." I will complete this story later.

If we have been wronged, we must forgive! Even if we don't feel like forgiving, we must forgive! If the offending party has not asked for forgiveness, still we must forgive!

Jesus is the perfect example. As He hung on the cross, no one was asking Christ's forgiveness; in fact, they were mocking and tormenting Him. Yet, Jesus said, "Father, forgive them." Therefore, forgiveness is not optional, it is mandatory! It is not an occasional action, it is a way of life!

Forgiving the person who has wronged you releases the Holy Spirit to bring conviction to the one causing you the problem. Nothing escapes the eyes of our Heavenly Father. He knows the intents, or motives, of the heart. The Holy Spirit is able to convict of sin, righteousness and judgment.

Now, back to our story! The lady in my office had been married for many years. Her husband had left her and was living with another woman. Having to care for herself and her family, she was put under difficult financial circumstances. Now she was in my office asking for healing from her paralysis.

The Holy Spirit caused me to ask her, "Have you forgiven your husband?"

"No! I can't! I hate him!" she sobbed, not able to control the tears.

"You must forgive him!" I continued. "This will cleanse your spirit of bitterness which may be preventing your healing. It will also release the hand of the Holy Spirit in his life."

After a while, she agreed to forgive her husband and return to pray and fast at Prayer Mountain. The following Sunday after one of our services, I heard a knock on my office door. I invited the person to enter. I noticed a man looking very grim walking in first, followed by a lady.

"Pastor, this is my husband whom we have been praying for." She was hardly able to control the tears of joy as she turned to her husband and said, "Please tell the pastor what happened."

"Pastor Cho, you think God can forgive me?" He continued, "I am a great sinner." Then, he told his story: "A week ago I started feeling very guilty as I was at home with the other woman. I could not stand the pain that I felt inside. Suddenly, I started to think of my wife and children whom I had abandoned. Not being able to relieve myself from the guilt that I felt, I thought of committing suicide. As Sunday approached, I decided to come to church, hoping to get forgiven and feel better. I then noticed my wife sitting across the auditorium. That is when I decided to ask her and God for forgiveness. Can God forgive me?"

"Yes, He can forgive you." I answered. Then I led him in the sinner's prayer and he accepted Jesus Christ as his Savior. What a joy it was to see the two reunited in Jesus Christ!

Later, as the woman continued to fast and pray, she was able to get up from her wheelchair and be healed. However, she had already been healed internally through forgiveness before being healed externally in divine healing.

I do not mean that everyone who is crippled or handicapped is suffering because of unforgiveness. Yet, many would be healed if they would only learn how to forgive.

If you, the reader, have a problem in forgiving someone, don't let pride take over, keeping you from obeying God's Word. Determine to go the extra mile, laying down your self-righteous attitude and forgiving that person! You will then experience a release of your hostilities and feel much better.

God resists the proud, but He gives more grace to the humble. Therefore, if you are having trouble with not having enough grace in your life, it could be that you are standing on your pride and not on the grace of God. What do you have to lose: except bitterness, resentment and possibly, ill health?

"And the prayer of faith shall save the sick, and the Lord shall raise him up; and if he have committed sins, they shall be forgiven him. Confess your faults one to another, and pray one for another, that ye may be healed . . ." (James 5:15–16).

Psychologists, medical doctors and psychiatrists now agree that the mental attitudes of their patients to a great degree control their success in healing.

Now is the time for the Body of Jesus Christ, the church, to be healed! God's attitude is shown in John's third epistle: "Beloved, I wish above all things that thou mayest prosper and be in health, even as thy soul prospereth" (3 John 2). The key to getting spiritual and material prosperity is linked to our soul (mind) prospering through forgiveness.

Therefore, fasting and prayer, combined with forgiveness, will cause a greater degree of health in the church. This will make the vehicle God has chosen to bring revival a healthy and useful tool in the hands of the Holy Spirit.

We have, in the latter portion of the twentieth century, a great challenge. It is also a great opportunity. What is needed is greater people—willing to forgive, sacrifice, obey and commit. I have made myself available to the Holy Spirit to do whatever is in my power to be an instrument of revival and church growth. Won't you join with me?

14

Waiting on the Lord

△

Meditation and prayer

Meditation is the act of contemplating or reflecting on something or someone. It demands discipline, since the mind tends to wander on many different things. It is an integral and important form of prayer. Since our actions are affected by our will, and since our will is to a great degree affected by our thinking; if we can therefore direct our thinking (contemplation), we can control our actions.

David prayed, "Let the words of my mouth, and the meditation of my heart be acceptable in thy sight, O Lord, my strength, and my redeemer" (Psa. 19:14).

God gave Joshua the secret to this success and prosperity: "This book of the law shall not depart out of thy mouth; but thou shalt meditate therein day and night, that thou mayest observe to do according to all that is written therein: for then thou shalt make thy way prosperous, and then thou shalt have good success" (Josh. 1:8). It is clear from this verse that God expected Joshua to meditate on something specific. He was to meditate on the Word of God. He was not told just to meditate on anything, but the strength of his mind was specifically directed to something concrete!

When you meditate, you must focus your mind clearly on the subject on which you desire to meditate. So often, Christians begin to meditate on the Lord, but they allow their minds to wander uncontrollably. Eventually, they fall asleep or get bored. The reason for this is that God expects us to meditate specifically on something, not just meditate on generalities.

To concentrate your mental faculties on a specific subject over a protracted period of time, you must delight in that thing. "But his delight is in the law of the Lord; and in his law doth he meditate day and night" (Psa. 1:2). Therefore, to meditate successfully on something, you must be motivated. You must see the benefit you will derive from the thing you are meditating on. If you delight yourself in the Word of God, then you will gladly meditate on it and receive greater knowledge and understanding. "My mouth shall speak of wisdom; and the meditation of my heart shall be of understanding" (Psa. 49:3).

David was motivated to praise the Lord continually in the Psalms because he allowed himself to meditate on God's goodness in his life: "My soul shall be satisfied as with marrow and fatness; and my mouth shall praise thee with joyous lips: when I remember thee upon my bed, and meditate on thee in the night watches. Because thou hast been my help, therefore in the shadow of thy wings will I rejoice" (Psa. 63:5–7). And again, "My meditation of him shall be sweet; I will be glad in the Lord" (Psa. 104:34).

The apostle Paul also saw the importance of meditation. Writing to his disciple Timothy, he told him to: "Neglect not the gift that is in thee . . . . Meditate upon these things; give thyself wholly to them; that thy profiting may appear to all" (1 Tim. 4:14–15). Timothy was therefore instructed to give himself totally to the ministry call given to him by the Holy Spirit. The way he could accomplish this total devotion was through meditation. Yet, again, he was commanded to meditate on *some*thing specifically, not just generally on *any*thing.

Waiting on the Lord △ 127

The prophet Isaiah prophesied that the way to maintain perfect peace was to continually meditate on the Lord: "Thou wilt keep him in perfect peace, whose mind is stayed on thee" (26:3).

When I prepare my sermons, I ask God to enlighten my mind to know the mind of the Holy Spirit, who wrote the Word of God. After I finish writing my outline, I then meditate on the message I am going to relate to God's people. From the introduction to the conclusion, through every one of my points, the Holy Spirit gives me fresh understanding of what the Word means and how to apply the Word to meet the needs of the thousands who will hear the message. Although I have hundreds of thousands in attendance on Sunday; although the message is rebroadcasted in several countries through the medium of television; I believe that the Holy Spirit knows the need of every individual and will meet that need through my Spirit-anointed message. By meditating, I will know what to say and when to say it. Later I learn of something that was said that met the specific need of someone hearing the message. How did I know exactly what to say? I didn't; but the Holy Spirit knew and communicated it to my mind while I was meditating on my sermon.

Not only do I meditate on my messages, but I also meditate on any new direction or opportunity that is before me. Some new avenue of ministry may look very appealing to the rational mind, but there may be pitfalls or potholes along the way that I may not know about; however, I trust the peace of God that I maintain in my heart. As I meditate on any important decision, the Holy Spirit directs me. When I am moving in God's will, I get that peace that is beyond understanding—since it is beyond understanding, it is also beyond too much explanation. When there is something that will hurt me or the work of the Lord, I know it because the Holy Spirit shows me by lifting that peace.

In order to have successful meditation, one must first get quiet before God. As one remains still, the confusion which surrounds all busy people departs and one is ready to meditate. I find that it often takes at least thirty minutes to get quiet before the Lord. This is why discipline is so important if one is going to be a successful prayer warrior. One cannot allow the internal conflicts to trouble his spirit. He cannot allow external problems to affect his peace. One must maintain a heart quiet before God if he is going to have genuine meditation.

Isaiah has a very natural break after the thirty-ninth chapter. It comes as a result of a change in direction for the prophet reflecting God's Word. As God finishes His judgments in chapter 39, He now begins to comfort Israel in the fortieth chapter. The fortieth chapter ends with divine principles: "He giveth power to the faint; and to them that have no might he increaseth strength. Even the youths shall faint and be weary, and the young men shall utterly fall: But they that wait upon the Lord shall renew their strength; they shall mount up with wings as eagles; they shall run, and not be weary; and they shall walk, and not faint" (40:29–31).

The prevailing principle in the verse just quoted is that natural strength is not enough to carry on the job before God's people. What is needed is strength that goes beyond youth and natural ability. Everyone who is willing to wait upon the Lord can be qualified to carry out the great task before them because the source of their strength is not natural but spiritual.

Today, many people are so busy that they have little time for prayer, much less time to wait before the Lord in meditation. Therefore, they cannot hear the inner voice of the Holy Spirit because it is not a loud voice. Elijah learned this:

"And he (Elijah) came thither unto a cave, and lodged there; and, behold, the word of the Lord came to him, and he said unto him, 'What doest thou here, Elijah?' And he said, 'I have been very jealous for the Lord God of hosts: for the children of Israel have forsaken thy covenant, thrown down thine altars, and slain thy prophets with the sword; and I, even I only, am left; and they seek my life, to take it away.' And he said, 'Go forth, and stand upon the mount before the Lord.' And, behold, the Lord passed by, and a great and strong wind rent the mountains, and brake in pieces the rocks before the Lord; but the Lord was not in the wind, and after the wind an earthquake; but the Lord was not in the earthquake! And after the earthquake a fire; but the Lord was not in the fire: and after the fire a still small voice. And it was so, when Elijah heard it, that he wrapped his face in his mantle, and went out, and stood in the entering in of the cave. And, behold, there came a voice unto him, and said, 'What doest thou here, Elijah?'" (1 Kings 19:9–13).

Elijah learned that his direction did not come in the loud manifestations of earthquake, fire or wind; but God directed him through the "still small voice."

The way to hear God's voice is to get still and meditate. If we are too busy to meditate, we are too busy to hear His voice! However, we are not to be casual about hearing the voice of the Lord. We must always remember that God has said everything doctrinally He will ever say in the Scripture. We will never hear anything from God that will ever contradict the revealed and inspired Bible! The canon of Scripture was closed with the last chapter of Revelation, which also includes the warning: "If any man shall add unto these things, God shall add unto him the plagues that are written in this book . . ." (Rev. 22:18).

Enjoying God's presence through meditation

One of the aspects of meditation that I particularly enjoy is what I call "taking a spiritual walk." Just as I enjoy the rare opportunities I get to take a casual walk without going in any specific direction, I enjoy meditating or waiting on the Lord without any specific purpose in mind. I simply sit in God's presence and enjoy Him. I don't have anything I desire, I just want Him. So I get alone and sit down in a comfortable chair, close my eyes and wait on the Lord. I may hear nothing. I may sense nothing. But I always feel refreshed after my spiritual stroll with my precious Lord. I find that this type of spiritual refreshment can last for hours.

C. Austin Miles wrote a hymn whose chorus reflects what I experience regularly:

And He walks with me, and He talks with me,
And He tells me I am His own;
And the joy we share, as we tarry there,
None other has ever known.

Enoch is described in Jude: "And Enoch also, the seventh from Adam, prophesied of these, saying: 'Behold the Lord cometh with ten thousands of his saints, To execute judgment upon all, and to convince all that are ungodly among them of all their ungodly deeds which they have ungodly committed, and of all their hard speeches which ungodly sinners have spoken against him'" (Jude 14–15). Yet, Genesis only says: "And Enoch walked with God after he begat Methuselah three hundred years, and begat sons and daughters: And all the days of Enoch were three hundred sixty and five years: And Enoch walked with God: and he was not; for God took him" (Gen. 5:22–24). What happened to Enoch?

Enoch was a prophet in the earliest days of man on earth. At that time, men still knew the stories about the garden: That is, Adam's experience with the Lord in the cool of the evening in the Garden of Eden. Enoch prophesied about a day that is yet to come: the second coming of Christ to execute judgment on the earth. Yet, in the midst of Enoch's ministry, he learned to walk with God. God enjoyed the pleasure of his company so much that the Bible says, "he was not." God took him to heaven so that he could enjoy him all of the time. He also is waiting for the second coming of Christ—when Enoch will be one of the ten thousand (or countless numbers) of the saints who will return with Christ, the righteous Judge.

I have developed a close fellowship with the Lord which has sharpened my spirit and caused me to overcome the attacks of Satan. Nothing is more important to me than that unrestricted time of fellowship I enjoy so much. For many of my members, they like to go to Prayer Mountain for this kind of communion and meditation. Others have a special place in their home that is quiet. Where you meditate is not as important as just meditating!

Part IV

Methods of Praying

Introduction

A

In this section, my objective is to give you, the reader, scripturally sound and practical methods to assist you in your prayer life. Having traveled throughout the world over many years, I am keenly aware of questions that have been asked about prayer everywhere I have been. Every area of the world has its own language, culture and practices; yet, we are all members of one body: the Body of Jesus Christ. Understanding how methodology can differ from one part of the world to another, it remains true that there are universal biblical principles that can be applied to all areas. For example, certain cultures, due to their particular climactic conditions, have a tendency to be more contemplative than others. Yet, we have all been given grace to overcome whatever natural proclivities we may have so that we may be true to the Word of God. I also find a universal desire among Christians for revival. Believing that the key to revival is prayer, I therefore desire to share methods that will help us toward that end.

15

Developing Persistence in Prayer (Learning How to Pray Longer)

A

"How can I pray longer than one or two hours?" a pastor asked me recently. After listening to one of my lectures on prayer, he was moved with a desire to pray more. However, he had been moved before. He had started a routine which only lasted a few weeks, then he settled back to his short prayer-time after the pressures of pastoring a congregation mounted. The answer to his question, also asked by many ministers and lay-Christians, caused me to include this chapter on developing persistence in prayer.

Normally, most believing Christians pray between thirty to sixty minutes daily. Since most live busy lives, the pressures of modern life have caused many to desire instant answers to quick prayers. Therefore, I find many buying books and listening to audio-cassette tapes designed to give formulas and short cuts to getting prayers answered. People are now accustomed to instant coffee, instant cures, tomorrow's paper the night before and the world news in ten minutes. Things today are capsulated whether they be vitamins or sermons. Instead of going out for a leisurely dinner with the family, an increasing number of families pull up to a fast food counter and eat in the car.

Christians have been affected by this modern sociological phenomenon as well. Popular in our churches in years past were beautiful hymns declaring the majesty of God. Now many churches have put away their hymnals and are using just chorus sheets. Not that the choruses are bad. But we should have both. We used to sing, "Sweet Hour of Prayer," now we are asking people to have "a word of prayer." Perhaps the reason we are not having revival in so much of the world today is that we are not willing to pray longer!

In learning how to pray, we must not be in a hurry. It has been said that God is omnipresent (everywhere at the same time), but God is never in a hurry. Therefore, we must learn to discipline ourselves to take the time to pray longer. We must learn how to wait in prayer until God answers.

As a busy pastor, I am under extreme time pressure. If a person were to write this book who had nothing more to do than pray, perhaps few would be challenged by it. However, I am a pastor of a 370,000-member church. I am president of Church Growth International. I must speak on television and radio regularly on two continents. Yet, I must pray! The methods that I use, I really use daily. I am not writing theories that I believe will work. The things which I write work daily in my life, causing me to pray longer.

As I have shared before, getting up early every morning helps me to have the time necessary to pray. I normally get up by 5:00 A.M. I physically get out of bed. If I were to pray in my bed, I might go back to sleep; so, it is important to change my physical location. Moving into my study, I sit before the Lord and begin to worship and thank Him for His goodness. David practiced entering God's gates in this way: "Enter into his gates with thanksgiving, and into his courts with praise: be thankful unto him, and bless his name" (Psa. 100:4).

After thanking, praising and worshiping God, I can ask His blessing on every appointment, counseling session and meeting I will have that day. In detail, I ask God's blessings upon my associates (I have over three hundred associate pastors); our missionaries (who are in forty countries); and my elders and deacons. I then inquire of the Lord for His direction on every decision. The psalmist told us: "I will instruct thee and teach thee in the way which thou shalt go: I will guide thee with mine eye" (Psa. 32:8).

After we develop a personal and intimate relationship with our Lord, He can direct us quietly and simply: "I will guide thee with mine eye." Yet, this does not happen overnight, it takes time. Depending on how much we desire to be guided, we will invest the necessary time to pray.

After praying for each department of my church, each government official and our national defense, I pray for my family, naming their needs clearly and specifically to our Lord. Then, using my imagination, I travel to Japan where we have an extensive ministry. I pray for our television outreach, which is increasingly leading more Japanese to Christ. As fellow Orientals, the Japanese accept my ministry much more readily than they accept American programs; therefore, our programs are having an impact on Japan. Yet, the resources necessary to continue this ministry are limited. Therefore, I ask God to meet every financial need in our Japanese office. God has promised me ten million Japanese souls by the end of this century. I keep reminding God of His promise and ask His strength and guidance to see this goal accomplished. I so intensely believe that ten million Japanese are going to bow their knees to Jesus Christ, I actually can visualize them in my mind.

Leaving the shores of Japan, I travel the great Pacific Ocean to America. I pray for the president, the Congress and the other institutions in the United States. I pray for the Christians in America that they may experience revival in their churches. I pray for our television outreach in America, believing that God will use it to bring revival. Then, I pray for the other thousands who send in their prayer requests. These are forwarded to me in Korea. Both the United States and Canada are key countries in the great revival which is coming world-wide. God therefore has burdened me to see revival in Canada and the United States.

I travel south and pray for Latin America. Having traveled throughout some of Latin America, I have been deeply moved and blessed by the beautiful people of that region. God is moving in some countries, but that region of the world has been targeted by the communists for a takeover. Therefore, prayers must be offered for peace for that region so the gospel can be preached and sinners saved before the end.

I then travel across the Atlantic Ocean and pray for Europe. I have been teaching in Europe for more than fifteen years. I love each country in which I have preached. Europe is the seedbed of the gospel in the West; yet, in most of that continent there is no sign of revival. However, I know that God wants to move in Europe and I intercede for them in the Holy Spirit. Eastern Europe is a particular concern to me because of the oppression and opposition which exists. God is most concerned about each Christian who is meeting secretly in Eastern Europe and I must pray for their safety and success.

Africa, Australia and New Zealand are also areas where God desires to move. I feel a special relationship to these areas because they are in my spirit in prayer.

Then there is my own continent of Asia. Of all the needy places on earth, Asia is the most needy in terms of the gospel. Of all the places that have never received the gospel, Asia has over 80 percent. I am therefore particularly burdened for my own continent. We have a ministry to China, which I cannot write about for obvious reasons, and my prayer then turns to them.

As you can see, just praying daily for all of the great needs in the Body of Christ world-wide will take at least half of my early morning prayer-time. Finally, I take time to pray for myself. Before I realize it, it is seven o'clock in the morning and I must prepare myself to go to my office.

During my morning hours, I feel the strength that early morning prayer has brought me. I can preach, feeling His divine anointing. I can counsel, sensing His wisdom. I can teach, experiencing His knowledge. Therefore, it is not I, but it is God working through me to accomplish His purpose.

In the afternoon, after lunch, I get quiet before the Lord again. Why? Because, as His ambassador, I need up-to-the-minute instructions from my headquarters. David said, "Evening, and morning, and at noon, will I pray, and cry aloud: and he shall hear my voice" (Psa. 55:17).

One of the biggest problems people have in prolonging their prayer lives is that they are not willing to repeat praying for the same thing daily. They think that praying over something once is enough. Yet, daily God gave Israel manna in the wilderness. Yesterday's manna did not last over twenty-four hours. So also we need daily communication with our Savior. We also eat, sleep and breathe every day. The meal we had yesterday will not satisfy today's need. The breath we took last second will have to be repeated over and over again or else we will die. Jesus said, "Give us this day our daily bread." He did not say that we should get bread so that we won't need to eat again.

At night, my day ends in prayer. I have so much to thank Him for because daily He proves His faithfulness to me. Tomorrow will bring new challenges which I will have the grace of God to succeed in. If I have failed in any way, I ask God for more grace and wisdom; if I have succeeded, I give Him the praise.

Life would not be the same without hours of daily prayer. No one knows what problems I would face if I did not pray daily. As the pastor of the largest church in the world, I know that Satan tries to destroy me daily. If he could tempt me to take a short cut in my prayer life, I would be vulnerable to his attacks. I therefore cannot afford to miss even one hour of my prayer time, for I know that this is the source of my inner strength.

Won't you pray with me that you be given greater desire, strength and discipline to pray longer? Think of the greater effectiveness of your life in ministry, business or school if you would dedicate yourself to prolong your prayer-time.

16

Praying in the Holy Spirit

A

"What is it then? I will pray with the spirit, and I will pray with the understanding also; I will sing with the spirit, and I will sing with the understanding also" (1 Cor. 14:15).

Paul testified, "I thank my God, I speak with tongues more than ye all" (1 Cor. 14:18). This he spoke to a church he was correcting on the overuse of spiritual manifestations. Therefore, Paul practiced praying in his prayer language more than anyone in the Corinthian church, yet he was motivated by the love of God.

Why should we pray in the Holy Spirit? Paul taught, "He that speaketh in an unknown tongue edifieth himself, . . ." (1 Cor. 14:4). Jude also restates this principle: "But ye, beloved, building up yourselves on your most holy faith, praying in the Holy Ghost" (Jude 20). Therefore, praying in your prayer language is the means by which you can build yourself up spiritually.

I find that my prayer language is a great spiritual blessing to me. If we could not benefit from praying in the Holy Spirit, God would have never given this precious gift to us. Jesus Christ said before He was ascended into heaven: "And these signs shall follow them that believe; in my name shall they cast out devils; they shall speak with new tongues" (Mark 16:17).

As a young Christian, I could not see the importance of tongues in my Christian life. However, the longer I believe in Jesus Christ, the more I feel the tremendous importance of tongues in my own personal Christian life. I spend a good deal of my prayer life praying in my spiritual language. Like Paul, I pray in the Spirit, and I pray with my understanding also.

In public, I would rather pray in a language which all can understand. Yet, in my personal prayer-time, I use my spiritual prayer language a great deal. The Scripture states: "For he that speaketh in an unknown tongue speaketh not unto men, but unto God: for no man understandeth him; howbeit in the Spirit he speaketh mysteries" (1 Cor. 14:2).

Since Paul says that no man can understand your prayer language except God, your prayer cannot be hindered by opposing spiritual forces, as Daniel experienced. Your spirit can communicate unhindered directly with the Father through the Holy Spirit.

Sometimes, I feel a burden of prayer; yet, I may not know exactly what I should pray for; or, I may not have exactly the words to express what I feel. This is the time that I enter my spiritual language and can pierce through my natural inability to articulate to God what I am feeling. I can go directly into my Father's presence in the Holy Spirit.

The word used for building in the original Greek language is OIKODOMEW, or placing one block on another. As in erecting a building, you can sense your faith actually being built as you pray in the Holy Spirit.

Knowing that it is important for my messages to build faith and hope in the hearts of thousands of people, I spend a good deal of time building my own faith level up by praying in the Holy Spirit.

I understand that many of my evangelical Christian friends have not used this important spiritual gift. However, they are not second-class Christians because they don't. In fact, I believe that the Holy Spirit today is causing all Christians to come closer together spiritually. We may not all agree, we may not all see the importance of using the spiritual prayer language, but we cannot discount its use in the New Testament. I could not write a book about prayer without honestly sharing with you what is for me a great spiritual help in prayer.

There is an internal struggle going on in the life of every Christian. The spirit is constantly warring against the flesh. By building yourself spiritually, you will find strength to overcome the flesh which is trying to drag you down.

Today I received a letter from a Korean construction technician in Singapore. He was lamenting how weak he was and determined many times not to smoke, use bad language and do any evil deed. So often, since he had become a Christian, he had tried but continued to fail. What could he do to strengthen himself spiritually? he asked. What could help this kind of weak Christian? The answer I gave him was the development of a spiritual prayer language. When he learns how to pray in the Holy Spirit, the Holy Spirit will cause him to be built up spiritually to the degree that he will be able to overcome all of the temptations of the flesh.

"Likewise the Spirit also helpeth our infirmities: for we know not what we should pray for as we ought: but the Spirit himself maketh intercession for us with groanings which cannot be uttered" (Rom. 8:26).

As I have just quoted, Paul states that the Holy Spirit Himself makes intercession for us! Since praying in the Holy Spirit is using our prayer language, the way to be strengthened, to help our infirmities, is praying in our prayer language. The Holy Spirit knows our spiritual need better than we do. However, He will use our own tongue to pray for our need. Praise the Lord for the Holy Spirit!

One of my cell leaders experienced an unusual event in prayer which underscores what I am sharing with you. As our cell leader locked the door to her apartment, she walked to the home where the meeting was being held. A couple of blocks from her home, she felt something unusual in her heart. She was deeply burdened. Falling on her knees, she began to pray. Soon she moved from her natural language into her prayer language. After a while, the burden started to lift, and she knew that she had been heard and the answer was on its way.

At the meeting, she preached her message under a heavy anointing of the Holy Spirit. After the meeting, she returned home to find that her home had been broken into. Looking for things of value, the thief had strewn clothes all over the floor. Yet, something strange had happened. Her jewelry and cash, which were not hidden, were untouched. Somehow, the thief had been blinded to the obvious things of value in her apartment. We believe that when she was praying, the Holy Spirit saw the need and caused her to pray. As the Holy Spirit was interceding for her, the thief was hampered from stealing anything of value. God saw and God answered!

During the war in Vietnam, many of our church's young men went to fight with their American allies in the jungles of that country. Many of their parents would come to me and say, "Pastor, we don't know how to pray or what to pray for. Please help us because we don't know the condition of our sons!" My response to them was, "Why don't we ask God to use our prayer language, since we don't know what to pray for?" Therefore we prayed: "Dear Heavenly Father, use our prayer language and pray through us for our children. Please meet the needs of our children today. You know where they are. You know their condition." Soon, we were all praying in our prayer language and we would continue to pray until the burden lifted. Sometimes, some of the parents would continue to pray in the Spirit for days, until the burden lifted.

I testify to the praise and glory of God that during the war in Vietnam, not one of our church boys died. The bullets may have been flying, but our sons were protected by the Holy Spirit!

This is why I do not neglect that which God has graciously given me. I ask you to pray about this important form of prayer. Ask God to show you how you can be protected, built up and strengthened by the Holy Spirit in a new way. For you who pray in the Holy Spirit, please do not quench the Spirit in your life! "In everything give thanks: for this is the will of God in Christ Jesus concerning you. Quench not the Spirit. Despise not prophesyings. Prove all things; hold fast that which is good" (1 Thess. 5:18–21).

To be a spiritual intercessor, we must have a desire to stand in the gap. Intercessor literally means to stand between. We must be willing to stand between the need and God, the only One able to meet the need.

We must also be willing to be used by the Holy Spirit in prayer at unexpected times and in unexpected places. We must be willing to be used by the Holy Spirit to pray for needs that we are not aware of naturally. The need may be in another part of the world, but the Holy Spirit may desire to use us to meet that need in prayer. God is looking for people who are willing to be used by God. To be a successful intercessor, you should also be willing to pray in the Holy Spirit.

17

The Prayer of Faith

△

Faith is the special ingredient that fills prayer with power and results. If we pray without faith, we are simply making sounds in the air. They never get further than the ceiling. The Scripture says, "But without faith it is impossible to please him; for he that cometh to God, must believe that he is, and that he is a rewarder of them that diligently seek him" (Heb. 11:6). In other words, when we come to God in prayer, we must come in an attitude of faith. God does not make faith in prayer optional, we must have faith in prayer in order for our prayer to be heard. Therefore, God will not hear prayer that is in doubt. He will only hear prayers that are in faith!

How can we develop the prayer of faith?

To help you develop faith in prayer, I wish to share with you three basic steps to use:

1. Our faith must be clearly directed toward a goal!

As I have stated before regarding prayer, our faith must be fixed on a definite and sure target. Just as a rocket fired from a missile launcher is set on a definite target, the computer being fixed on the proper coordinates, so also our prayers of faith must be targetted.

A man asked me, "Pastor Cho, please pray that the Lord will bless me." My response was, "What kind of blessing do you want? There are thousands of blessings in the Bible. You must be specific in order to get answered. If you are not, how will you know when God has answered you?"

If you have a financial need, don't just ask God, "Lord, I need some money, so please help me!" We must pray, "Lord, I need $10,000 for my unpaid bills, and I ask You to please send me $10,000 so that I may pay these bills so that no shame may come to Your servant." Therefore, if you need $10,000 ask for that amount specifically! If you need $589.50 don't ask for around $600, ask for the exact amount you need!

God has always responded to direct and specific prayers. Everything He does has a plan and purpose. In Genesis 1 and 2, we are told that God created within specific time frames called days. When He told Moses to build a Tabernacle, He gave him clear directions. Moses was not left to decide whether he would build the tent around twenty cubits (the length between the elbow and the tip of the finger) long; no, he was told exactly how long and how wide. Therefore, God is a precise God and He expects us to pray precisely!

Faith is the substance of *things!* Faith is not the substance of generalities, but of definite things hoped for. And faith is the evidence of *things* hoped for—again very specific (see Heb. 11:1).

2. The prayer of faith must lead us into visions and dreams!

The prophet Joel said, "And it shall come to pass afterward, that I will pour out my spirit upon all flesh; and your sons and your daughters shall prophesy, your old men shall dream dreams, and your young men shall see visions" (2:28). How do the young see visions and the old dream dreams? They are able to do so because visions and dreams are the language of the Holy Spirit.

When referring to the faith of Abraham, Paul said, ". . . before him whom he believed, even God, who quickeneth the dead, and calleth those things which be not as though they were" (Rom.

4:17). Abraham's faith is amplified in Romans not only describing the nature of Abraham's faith, but also the nature of his God on whom his faith rested. He was able to believe in a God who was able to create and impart a vision and a dream concerning His promise—to the degree that what was not obvious to the eye was still real, by faith. Therefore, Abraham "staggered not" at the promise of God. Because God said it, Abraham believed—not looking at his own biological incapability to produce offspring at the age of one hundred years. Abraham had the reality in his visions and dreams.

Visualization is something which is now just being understood by psychologists and physiologists. Recent reports show that new athletic training includes visualization. In other words, an athlete is asked to visualize in his imagination winning the race, leaping over the pole, or throwing the javelin further than his previous ability has been able to produce. By doing this, the athlete's body gears itself to success. If he has a poor mental image of his performance, the athlete does more poorly than normal; but if he visualizes success, then he is able to compete with unusual success.

So it is in prayer, that is the prayer of faith. We must learn to visualize the results before God brings them—calling those things which are not as if they were. If you long for a child to bring happiness to your childless home, then begin to see that child in your visions and dreams. You and your husband should not only pray and ask for the child, but begin to see a new baby boy or girl, bright and healthy, filling your home with happiness. At night, fill your heart with that dream. In the morning, let that be your vision. Just as Abraham and Sarah were able to see their children by faith, not counting the fact that both were way beyond the child-bearing stage of life, you too can see the child of your faith-prayer come into being.

Abraham was told to look at the stars and count them at night. So would his offspring be. His imagination was overwhelmed with the fulfillment of his faith, becoming pregnant with God's promise. In the day, Abraham was told to get on top of a mountain and look to the east, north, south and west—everything he could see would be his possession. Therefore, his imagination was again made pregnant with God's promise, his vision being used by God to build faith.

Man still knows little about how his mind and body work. He has traveled to outer space, but he knows so little of his inner space. If man knows so little about his body and mind, he knows even less about how his spirit works. Visualization is being spoken by man as a new discovery; but God has revealed this principle throughout the entire Scripture.[5]

God has promised to give you the desires of your heart. As I referred to this in the second section, "Prayer Is Petition," your desires must be in line with the Word of God, the Bible!

For example, if a Christian girl prays for a young man to marry and meets a man who is not a Christian, that man is not the answer to her prayer. Why? The Word of God already says, "Be ye not unequally yoked together with unbelievers: for what fellowship hath righteousness with unrighteousness and what communion hath light with darkness?" (2 Cor. 6:14). Therefore, no matter how she prays for that young man to be her husband, the Word of God has dictated the fact that God will not hear that prayer. She may pray specifically; she may use visions and dreams in her imagination; she may claim all of the promises; but God only responds to those prayers in accordance with the revealed Word of God, the Bible!

God is the God of the eternal now! He sees the end from the beginning. The faith that God responds to is the "now" faith mentioned in the first verse of Hebrews 11. When we pray in faith, we move into God's fourth dimensional realm of *now* faith. We see the results of God's promise to us as already done. We don't faint because of the circumstances which might seem impossible, but we come into the rest of God. That is, we stand firm, not wavering, knowing that God is faithful to do exceedingly abundantly more than we can ask or think.

---

[5]Read: *Fourth Dimension*, vol. II.

Do not put off God's answer into the future: "someday God will answer me!" We must call those things which be not as though they were. Abram's name was changed to Abraham (father of many) before his first son was born by his wife Sarah. Can you imagine the reaction of all who knew this powerful man? They must have shaken their heads, wondering why this old man would change his name without having the results of his promise. Yet Abraham's faith did not waver. He had learned to move into the "now" faith of God and call those things which were not as though they were already.

Abraham is called the father of faith because he experienced such dynamic faith which became an example for us all: "Now, it was not written for his (Abraham's) sake alone, that it (faith) was imputed to him, but for us also, . . ." (Rom. 4:23–24). We must learn from Abraham, in learning the prayer of faith!

3. To pray in faith, we must remove all obstacles that may negate God's answer!

The prayer of faith requires us to continue praying until we have the assurance in our hearts that God has heard us and the answer is on its way. "So then, faith cometh by hearing, and hearing by the word of God" (Rom. 10:17). In the original Greek manuscript, there is no definite article: "the." Therefore, this verse could better be translated: "faith comes by hearing (*akouo:* understanding) and hearing by a word from God." Faith is released when we pray, when we are given understanding in our hearts that God has heard and we receive His assurance (a word) that the answer is on its way. If we stop praying before that assurance, then we may not have generated sufficient faith to get our prayer answered.

We must also watch our confession! In the ninth verse of Romans 10, confession is linked to faith. So often, Christians negate the answer to their prayers because they begin to confess negative statements: "I prayed, but I don't think God will do it!" Never try to work on God's pity by your negative confession. God does not respond to pity, but He does respond to faith. God cannot be manipulated by self-pity: "Nobody seems to care about me!" or "I know I will be ruined!" Clear out all of the self-pity and begin to move in faith! Your attitude may determine the level of faith in which you pray. If your confession is negative it reveals that your heart is also negative! For out of our hearts our mouths speak.

A positive confession will cause you to praise God for the answer, even before you see it! You will wake up in the morning knowing that God has heard you and you confess with your mouth praise and thanksgiving. This will build your faith and will cause the hand of God to move on your behalf.

We must clear all of the sin out of our lives to move in the prayer of faith!

"If our hearts condemn us not then have we confidence toward God. And whatsoever we ask, we receive of him, because we keep his commandments, and do those things that are pleasing in his sight" (1 John 3:21).

If you have sin in your life, confess it to the Father quickly! Don't wait till the morning! Do it now! Clean your heart before God so that there might be a clear channel of prayer between you and your Heavenly Father: "If we confess our sins he is faithful and just to forgive us our sins and to cleanse us from all unrighteousness" (1 John 1:9).

God can keep every obstacle of sin, bitterness, hatred or fear from blocking the measure of faith that has been given to us. That measure of faith can grow and develop so that we may pray in faith. Now is the time to begin to pray in faith! The results of this kind of prayer will be miraculous: "And the prayer of faith shall save the sick, and the Lord shall raise him up; and if he have committed sins, they shall be forgiven him" (James 5:15).

18

Listening to God's Voice

△

Prayer is a dialogue, not a monologue. To pray effectively, we must listen to God as well as speak. Since we have been called by God into a loving relationship, we must see the importance of what that kind of relationship entails. Whether hearing God's Word in a better understanding of the Scripture or His divine direction for our lives, knowing how to listen to God is extremely important.

To listen to God's voice, we must have the proper attitude. "If a man will do his will, he shall know of the doctrine, whether it be of God, or whether I speak of myself" (John 7:17). In this verse, Jesus shows us the importance of a willing attitude regarding the will of God. Therefore, if we are not willing to do the will of God, we can't hear His voice clearly. Our desire to listen to God's voice must be couched within a willing attitude. Why should God speak to someone who is not willing to obey?

Another important principle in listening to God is having "an ear to hear." In Luke, Jesus told His disciples, "Let these sayings sink down into your ears; for the Son of man shall be delivered into the hands of men" (Luke 9:44). The disciples did not understand what Jesus said, although they heard it physically: "But they understood not this saying, and it was hid from them, that they perceived it not: and they feared to ask him of that saying" (Luke 9:45).

Why didn't the disciples understand what was clearly spoken to them? They did not have an ear to hear. As long as Jesus performed miracles, manifesting the power of the future kingdom, they were willing to understand at least the temporal implications of what Jesus taught. However, when they were told that they might lose their Messiah and Lord, they did not want to hear this, so they did not understand.

Educators have discovered when studying cognition (the mental process by which knowledge is acquired) that a student comprehends and retains best what he is motivated to learn. If the student is familiar with the subject matter, he will understand better than if he is not. If the student views that which is said to be of importance to his needs, he will listen more attentively. The disciples were not interested in listening to the possibility that Jesus would be taken by His enemies, therefore they did not listen.

Thus, having an ear to hear is to have the capacity to understand what has been said through having the proper attitude: obedience. If we don't sincerely want to do His will, we will not have the capacity to listen to God.

"He that hath an ear, let him hear what the Spirit saith unto the churches" (Rev. 3:6). This verse is repeated several times in chapters 2 and 3 of Revelation. The verse implies that we cannot hear what the Spirit is speaking unless we have a hearing ear. Not that we don't want to hear, but we must have the capacity to hear.

When we listen to the voice of God, He often corrects our wrong attitudes. He counsels us and gives us clear direction. If we have sinned, the Holy Spirit is quick to convict us of that sin and lead us back to the place where that sin was committed.

How do we develop the "hearing ear" to hear what the Holy Spirit is speaking to us? We must develop obedience to what we already know to be God's will. Why should God direct us if we have not obeyed what we already know God has directed us to do?

If there is sin in our lives, keeping us from obeying God, then we must quickly confess that sin and get it under the blood of Christ. This wipes the slate clean of all problems and causes us to come back to a loving relationship with Jesus Christ, capable of hearing His voice.

In listening to God, timing is most important!

God can speak to us, but we must know His timing. Knowing the timing of God takes discipline and patience: "The Lord hath given me the tongue of the learned, that I should know how to speak a word in season to him that is weary: he wakeneth morning by morning, he wakeneth mine ear to hear as the learned" (Isa. 50:4).

The context of this important verse is very important in knowing how to listen to God and move in His timing. Isaiah 50 begins by showing the sad state of Israel. Then God asks the rhetorical question: why? The answer is that when God wanted to visit Israel with blessing, He could not find a man who was available to be used. Then, we read the verse just quoted which prophetically has to do with the coming of the Messiah. Yet, the divine principle remains true for all who are desirous of hearing and obeying the voice of God. We must be disciplined (learned), then we must not only know the right word, but we must speak and obey in the right season.

The apostle Paul desired to preach in Asia. He very much wanted to share the matchless gospel of Jesus Christ in that needy part of the world. Yet the Holy Spirit did not allow Paul to go. He would not allow Paul to travel to Bythinia, so he ended up in Troas. At night the Lord directed him to Europe. This was the will of God. Thousands of years later, the gospel is preached in Asia—timing is crucial!

Many years ago, I was with a man of faith who had founded the first Christian television station in America. He was already on radio in California. While in his home, he persuaded me as to the necessity of having a Christian radio station in Korea. We made all of the arrangements, buying the expensive equipment and hiring the proper personnel. Yet I was not able to get the proper permit. I continuously prayed to God, but to no avail. It was not the right time. Today, my television and radio ministries cover Korea. The right time has come!

Therefore, be willing to obey; keep the right spiritual attitude; obey what you know already to be the will of God; and begin to listen attentively when you pray. The timing to your thoughts may not be perfect, but God will lead you in the way you should go. Even if it takes time, His direction is sure. "So shall my word be that goeth out of my mouth: it shall not return unto me void, but it shall accomplish that which I please, and it shall prosper in the thing whereto I sent it" (Isaiah 55:11).

God wants men and women with ears to hear what the Holy Spirit is saying to the church. Yet, the problem is not that God has stopped speaking; but, rather that we are not listening.

At the center of importance in listening to God is the recognition that God is a loving Father and we are His children through Jesus Christ our Lord.

As the father of three sons, I have a special appreciation for this important relationship we have with God. Although all three of my sons are similar in looks, they are each very different in personality. Each one of my sons has a distinctive way in which he listens and comprehends. Since my sons are of three different age groups, each one has to be addressed in a different way. It is my responsibility to communicate with them in a way they can understand. I do not speak to my youngest in the same way I speak to my oldest son. Our Heavenly Father does the same thing.

He desires to communicate with us even more than we desire to communicate with Him. He knows each one of our spiritual levels and will speak to us accordingly.

His Word is directed to us in various ways. Jeremiah prophesied, "'Is not My word like a fire?' says the Lord, 'And like a hammer that breaks the rocks in pieces?'" (Jer. 23:29).

Therefore, the Word of God can be directed powerfully to us like a fire, kindling response; or like a hammer, breaking all opposition. Yet the Word of God can be directed to our minds rather than to our emotions, "Come now, and let us reason together . . ." (Isa. 1:18, NKJV).

Whichever way God chooses to speak to us, we must learn to listen, remembering always to judge what we hear by the revealed Word of God, the Bible. The apostle John was particularly concerned about this when he wrote:

"Now he who keeps his commandments abides in him, and he in him. And by this we know that he abides in us, by the Spirit whom he has given us. Beloved, do not believe every spirit, but test the spirits, whether they are of God; because many false prophets have gone out into the world" (1 John 3:24–4:1, NKJV).

The Holy Spirit, therefore, is able to direct us into a spiritual sensitivity whereby we are able to test (judge) what we hear, distinguishing between God's direction and human or Satanic voices. How are we directed by God? We abide in Him, keeping His commandments. Just as a bank teller is able to judge between counterfeit notes and real notes because he handles the real, so also, we are able to discern the voice of God because we are abiding in Him in obedience.

In Matthew, we read: "Then if any man shall say unto you, 'Lo, here is Christ, or there'; believe it not. For there shall arise false Christs, and false prophets, and shall show great signs and wonders; insomuch that, if it were possible, they shall deceive the very elect" (24:23–24).

As we approach the last days, there will be more and more false prophecy in this world. Satan will try to deceive the church with many voices. Yet, those who learn to listen to God will not be deceived because they will know the difference between God speaking and counterfeit voices. As they learn to hear the voice of God, they cannot be fooled by other voices. It is increasingly important to learn how to test the spirits, being able to distinguish between God and the devil.

Jesus continues to describe the conditions in the world at the end of this age when He states: "But as the days of Noah were, so also will the coming of the Son of Man be. For as in the days before the flood, they were eating and drinking, marrying and giving in marriage, until the day that Noah entered the ark, and did not know until the flood came, and took them all away, so also will the coming of the Son of man be" (Matt. 24:37–39, NKJV).

The time before the second coming of Jesus Christ is called the last days. Those days are described in the verses just quoted. The last days will be similar to the days in which Noah built his ark. As the day of judgment approached, people continued to act as if nothing was happening. They were not conscious of the times they were living in. So also, people today are going about their normal business not knowing that the end of the age is near. They are not listening to the voice of God and will not be ready when the Lord comes.

How important is it to be in anointed communion with the Holy Spirit as the second coming approaches? The answer to this important question is found in Matthew:

"Then the kingdom of heaven shall be likened to ten virgins who took their lamps and went out to meet the bridegroom. Now five of them were wise, and five were foolish. Those who were foolish took their lamps and took no oil with them, but the wise took oil in their vessels with their lamps. But while the bridegroom was delayed, they all slumbered and slept. And at midnight a cry was heard: 'Behold, the bridegroom is coming; go out to meet him!' Then all those virgins arose and trimmed their lamps. And the foolish said to the wise, 'Give us some of your oil, for our lamps are going out.' But the wise answered, saying, 'No, lest there should not be enough for us and you; but go rather to those who sell, and buy for yourselves.' And while they went to buy, the bridegroom came, and those who were ready went in with him to the wedding; and the door was shut" (Matt. 25:1–10, NKJV).

By learning to listen to God, we will know what the Lord is doing: "Surely the Lord God does nothing, unless he reveals his secret to his servants the prophets" (Amos 3:7). By learning to listen to God, we will not be caught unaware at the Lord's coming.

As we learn how to abide in Christ, through the Holy Spirit, we will not allow our oil to run short; but we will be vigilant in waiting for the second coming of Christ.

We are living in a day when most Christians throughout the world are not conscious of the lateness of the hour. It is therefore imperative that we learn to listen to the voice of God daily!

19

The Importance of Group Prayer

A

When I pray alone, I can only exercise my own individual faith. Yet, when I pray in a group, with my brothers and sisters in Christ, the power of our faith is increased geometrically.

Moses told Israel that one could chase a thousand, yet two could put ten thousand to flight (see Deut. 32:30). The secret that Moses was referring to, a geometric and not an arithmetic increase to two standing together, was the presence of The Rock in their midst. Jesus stated the same thing when He told His disciples that where there were two or three gathered in His name, He would be in their midst (Matt. 18:20). More than one Christian gathering in the name of Christ causes there to be an automatic manifestation of the Body of Christ. This releases the promise: What we bind on earth is bound in heaven. This promise was not just made to Peter, but it was made to the Christian community standing together in faith (see Matt. 18:18).

Between the years 1969 to 1973, I went through the worst trial of my life. I thought I would surely drown in the waters of anguish which surrounded me at that time. We had just started building our present sanctuary with 10,000 seats and a high rise apartment building at the same time—and we did not have enough money.

The dollar being devalued caused a monetary crisis in Korea. The oil embargo pulled us further down into a recession. People in our church lost their jobs and our income plummeted. In the midst of all of this, our building costs skyrocketed because of the inflation which ensued. With my natural eyes I could see only one thing: bankruptcy.

I started to pray in the dark and damp unfinished basement of our new church. Soon, others began to join me in prayer and, together, our prayers reached the throne of heaven and we were delivered. As we completed the building, we saw the importance of group prayer. Thousands combined their faith to bring to pass the miracle that is now called the largest church in the history of Christianity.

Recently, Dr. Billy Graham and I met to pray and talk about reaching Japan with the gospel. In Amsterdam, Holland, Dr. Graham said, "Christianity has not grown significantly in Japan in the last two hundred years." He told me that during his large crusade in Osaka, a Japanese leader told him that the gospel has never really been made clear and relevant to the Japanese people. I am now praying for ten million Japanese Christians to bend their knees to Jesus Christ for salvation within the century. My entire church is praying as one man toward that end. We have established a clear pattern, goal and method. We believe that the time is now for Japan!

Out of 120 million Japanese people, there are only approximately 400 thousand Catholics and 300 thousand Protestant Christians. The Japanese are mainly a secular society, wealth and power being their aim. What can break the resistance to the gospel that has been in Japan for hundreds of years? The answer is persistent and united group prayer for that nation.

Jesus promised, "Again I say unto you, that if two of you shall agree on earth as touching any thing that they shall ask, it shall be done for them of my Father which is in heaven. For where two or three are gathered together in my name, there am I in the midst of them" (Matt. 18:19–20).

Last year on New Year's Day, I read that 80 million Japanese visited heathen shrines to pay homage to idols. This clearly shows the force that has bound this nation for so many years. When we in our church pray for the nation of Japan, we are praying for one of the strongest bastions of Satan. Although the Japanese people are very polite and civil, they are still caught in the devil's web without knowing it. However, I believe that God is able and I have complete confidence that what we bind in prayer on this earth, is also bound in the spirit world in heaven. Nothing will stop us from gaining the spiritual victory in Japan through prayer! Please, join with me in praying for revival for Japan.

If the geometric progression of faith holds true, that is, if one can chase one thousand and two can put ten thousand to flight, then, can you imagine how many demons we can chase in faith if you join your prayers with our 370 thousand believers in Korea for Satan to be bound over the nation of Japan! The victory is ours in Christ! Amen!

What can hinder group prayer?

Matthew tells an important story which underscores the only hindrance to faith and power:

"Now it came to pass, when Jesus had finished these parables, that he departed from there. And when he had come to His own country (Nazareth), He taught them in their synagogue, so that they were astonished and said, 'where did this man get this wisdom and these mighty works? Is this not the carpenter's son: is not his mother called Mary? And his brothers James, Joses, Simon, and Judas? And his sisters, are they not all with us? Where then did this man get all these things?'

"So they were offended at him. But Jesus said to them, 'A prophet is not without honor except in his own country and in his own house.' And he did not do many mighty works there because of their unbelief" (Matt. 13:53–58, NKJV).

Unbelief hindered an entire town from seeing the power of God through the Son of God, Jesus Christ. Unbelief is the opposite of faith. It blocks faith from operating, so that the faith necessary to pray effectively is hindered.

The disciples experienced unbelief when they tried to cast out demons unsuccessfully: "Then came the disciples to Jesus apart, and said, 'Why could not we cast him out?' And Jesus said unto them, 'Because of your unbelief: for verily I say unto you, if ye have faith as a grain of mustard seed, ye shall say unto this mountain, Remove hence to yonder place; and it shall remove; and nothing shall be impossible unto you'" (Matt. 17:19–20).

Therefore, when opposing the forces of Satan, there cannot be unbelief present. Unbelief will break the power of the group if it is allowed to be present when prayer is going on.

The Scripture teaches us that Abraham received the strength to produce Isaac because he did not allow unbelief in his heart (see Rom. 4:20). Paul also stated that it was due to unbelief that Israel was cut off from the living tree of faith (see Rom. 11:20).

Hebrews gives a grave warning concerning unbelief: "Beware, brethren, lest there be in any of you an evil heart of unbelief in departing from the living God; but exhort one another daily, while it is called 'Today,' lest any of you be hardened through the deceitfulness of sin. For we have become partakers of Christ if we hold the beginning of our confidence steadfast to the end" (Heb. 3:12–14).

Unbelief creeps insidiously into the heart creating a heart which Hebrews call evil. Just as faith builds power in prayer, unbelief destroys that power. It is like a cancer that must be cut out completely!

Paul warns the Corinthian Christians not to be associated with people of unbelief (see 2 Cor. 6:14).

Jairus was a ruler of the synagogue who asked Jesus to come and pray for his daughter. As Jesus was walking to Jairus's house, a large crowd gathered to see what would happen. A woman who had spent all of her money on doctors lunged at Christ but was just able to touch the hem of His garment. As she touched Him, the issue of blood that she had experienced for many years was healed. Jesus, feeling the virtue flowing out from His body asked, "Who touched me?" The story in Mark 5 continues as Jesus told her, "Daughter, your faith has made you well" (v. 34). After saying this, a man came to tell the leader of the synagogue that his daughter had died. Jesus' response was: "Do not be afraid; only believe" (v. 36).

The story climaxes as Jesus approached the house where the dead girl was being mourned: "And he permitted no one to follow him except Peter, James, and John the brother of James. Then he came to the house of the ruler of the synagogue, and saw a tumult and those who wept and wailed loudly. When he came in, he said to them, 'Why do you make this commotion and weep? The child is not dead, but sleeping.' And they laughed him to scorn. But when he had put them all out, he took the father and mother of the child, and those who were with him, and entered where the child was lying" (Mark 5:37–40, NKJV).

We must see that Jesus was very careful whom He allowed to accompany Him into the house. He only wanted the disciples who had no unbelief to be with Him as He raised the dead girl back to life. He also would not allow the professional mourners to stay. Their unbelief could have also blocked the faith necessary to perform this notable miracle. If Jesus therefore was careful about whom He allowed to pray with Him, should not we be also?

Therefore, it is extremely important that in our group prayer we block all unbelief from being manifested. In our church we first build faith through Bible study and teaching, before we join together in group prayer. The Truth casts out unbelief and God's Word is the Truth! Group prayer can be hindered by unbelief; but that unbelief can be removed in the name of Jesus Christ the Lord.

Although God listens to our individual prayers, group prayer is important, especially when we are binding the forces of Satan.

Part V

The Powerful Prayer Is Based on the Blood Covenant in Christ Jesus

20

Powerful Prayer

△

The prayer that will powerfully combat the forces of Satan must be based on the blood covenant of Jesus Christ! This is a sure foundation on which we can build our faith in order to pray effectively. No other biblical foundation exists that will give us the necessary understanding which will guide us during moments of testing and doubt. The Word of God, the Scripture, is the basis of our understanding of what the covenant is and its supreme importance to every Christian. Before we understand how this covenant of grace is the foundation of our prevailing prayer, we must understand the nature of the covenant.

What is a covenant?

A covenant is a mutual contract between individuals, and especially between kings and rulers. Abraham made a covenant with Abimelech (Gen. 21:27). Joshua made a covenant with God's people (Josh. 24:25). Jonathan made a covenant with the house of David (1 Sam. 20:16). Ahab made a covenant with Benhadad (1 Kings 20:34). Therefore, we must base our understanding of what a covenant is on the scriptural record of contracts or agreements which had to be lived up to.

God's relationship with man has also been based on a covenant. From God's relationship with Adam in the Garden of Eden to God's relationship with the church in the New Covenant, God has always specified what the responsibilities of each party were in His dealings with us. If we would live up to our end of the agreement, then God would live up to His. If we broke the agreement then the proper and justified results of our breaking our contract would ensue. Therefore, in God's covenants with man there have always been specifically named parties or principles, mutual stipulations or promises, and specified conditions.

The parties

In the covenant made through the blood of Christ, or the New Covenant, the parties are: God Himself and fallen mankind. Man through his original sin, the sin of Adam, fell from the grace and favor of God. Therefore, he is living out of fellowship with his Creator and is lost in the muck and mire of sin. Man is not a sinner because he sins, but he sins because essentially he is a sinner. Motivated by pure, unprovoked and unmerited love, God sent His only begotten Son, Jesus Christ, to assume man's nature. His purpose was to live a perfect, sinless life within that nature, forever proving the ability that man was given originally to live above sin. Jesus Christ then suffered the price of man's sin, death on the cross. Through that atoning death, God's wrath was satisfied and access to God was made available for man.

In God's covenant with Israel, Moses acted as the mediator of that covenant. In other words, Moses was given the responsibility to explain the implications of the covenant to the people. In the new blood covenant of Christ, He is the mediator of that covenant through the record which He left behind for the benefactors of the new agreement to follow. Hebrews views the two covenants and judges the new one to be better, due to the promises made by the mediator: God performs the word, man is the beneficiary.

Yet, in reality and under closer scrutiny, the covenant is really between the Father and the Son; in that, the Father promised the Son an inheritance and a kingdom which He fulfilled when He raised Christ up from the dead.

In Psalm 40, Hebrews 10, John 17:4 and Galatians 4:4, God reveals the pre-advent nature of Christ's work on earth. These as well as many other references clearly show the eternal plan or agreement between the Father and the Son which resulted in redemption.

The promises by Christ to the Father

The Son's part of the agreement was:

1. To prepare a proper and lasting habitation on earth for God. The Lord was never satisfied with the tabernacle of Moses, which spoke of things to come. He was never satisfied with the temples built by Solomon or Herod. He desired a place of continual and mutual habitation so that all might view and appreciate the revealed glory. Therefore, Jesus Christ would prepare this habitation in the church. He also would prepare a Body through which God could perform His divine purposes in the earth, Christ Himself being the head of that Body. This Body would be perfect and without blemish, just as Adam's original body was perfect. However, the new Body would be better because it would be comprised of millions of people throughout the world and it would never disobey because the head is the Son Himself.

2. The Son was to give the Holy Spirit without measure to the new family on earth, the church. The Holy Spirit had come partially on human flesh in the past causing men to prophesy, perform miracles and reveal the nature and will of God. Yet, the new promise would give the Holy Spirit in fullness. By giving Him to redeemed mankind in this way, the church would be able to have sufficient grace to accomplish the will of God, not out of duty but out of desire. The Holy Spirit would also be able to reverse the effects of sin on human nature and would adorn the Body of Christ with beauty, strength and holiness.

3. That He would return to His Father and sit with Him on His throne, making intercession for the fulfillers of His will. In doing so, the effects of bruising the head of Satan would culminate in the total destruction of the devil's kingdom and the annihilation of all evil from the earth.

The promises by the Father to Christ

1. The Father would deliver the Son from the power of death. Others had died and been raised from the dead for a while, but later they too had died. Yet, no one, from Adam till Christ, had ever died and been raised to live forever. In doing this, the Father not only raised the Son, but broke the power of death itself. Paul calls the power of death the greatest power to be destroyed (see 1 Cor. 15:26). Therefore, by destroying the power of death, all authority was given to Christ in heaven and on earth.

2. The Father would grant Christ the ability to give the Holy Spirit in fullness to whomever He would. By having this authority, He could give the ability to members of His Body to perform the will of the Father.

3. That the Father would seal and protect all that came to Christ through the Holy Spirit.

4. That the Father would give Him an inheritance comprised of people from all nations from the earth and that His kingdom or dominion would be forever and ever.

5. That through the extension of Christ as the Head of the Church, His Body would be able to attest to all principalities and powers the eternal and manifold wisdom of the Father, justifying the creation of God's love mankind for all eternity.

The condition

The condition under which the covenant between the Father and Son took place was that the Son would come in the form and nature of man, subject to all the same temptations and not relying on His divine nature. He would overcome every test the same way man can overcome, through the power of the Holy Spirit.

Christ would also submit Himself to death, even the ignominious death of the cross. Christ would shed His precious and sinless blood that would forever seal those who would believe in Him.

Christ, being the legal second party to the eternal and better new covenant, having fulfilled all His promises, having received the promises of the Father and having met all of the conditions has now clearly established the access that we have to the Father in prayer.

In other words, we have a right, a legal right, to approach the Father in prayer.

Why is this important?

Satan no longer has access to the Father to accuse man as he did in Job:

"Now there was a day when the sons of God came to present themselves before the Lord, and Satan also came among them. And the Lord said to Satan, 'From where do you come?' So Satan answered the Lord and said, 'From going to and fro on the earth, and from walking back and forth on it.' Then the Lord said to Satan, 'Have you considered my servant Job, that there is none like him on the earth, a blameless and upright man, one who fears God and shuns evil?' So Satan answered the Lord and said, 'Does Job fear God for nothing? Have You not made a hedge around him, around his household, and around all that he has on every side? You have blessed the work of his hands, and his possessions have increased in the land. But now, stretch out Your hand and touch all that he has, and he will surely curse You and Your face!' So the Lord said to Satan, 'Behold, all that he has is in your power; only do not lay a hand on his person.' Then Satan went out from the presence of the Lord" (Job 1:6–12, NKJV).

This story reveals how Satan had access to heaven and was able to accuse both God and righteous Job. He accused God because he said that the only reason Job served Him was because he was blessed—God was not fair. He accused Job, in that he stated that Job had the ability to curse God if all his possessions were taken away. The devil is and has always been the great accuser!

Christ, who saw the devil fall originally (Luke 10:18), reveals an aspect of His redemptive success in blocking all access to heaven by Satan: "And I heard a loud voice saying in heaven, 'Now is come salvation, and strength, and the kingdom of our God, and the power of his Christ: for the accuser of our brethren is cast down, which accused them before our God day and night. And they overcame him by the blood of the Lamb, and by the word of their testimony; and they loved not their lives unto the death'" (Rev. 12:10–11).

Therefore, Satan no longer has access to God, accusing His people continually. However, Satan still accuses us to ourselves in our own minds. He tells us that we are not worthy to pray. He continually puts thoughts in our minds that we don't have the right of access to the Throne of Grace from which we can find strength in time of need. Therefore, it is extremely important, particularly when are are battling the devil in prayer, that we realize that the effectiveness of our prayers is based on the blood covenant in the shed blood of Jesus Christ. We can call the devil a liar and the father of lies. We can overcome every thought that is not of God. We can bind every negative, accusing and self-depleting word that comes into our minds, trying to destroy our self-image. This we can do because the legal right to access has been purchased.

Therefore, come to God boldly! If you don't exercise your legal right of entry before the Father, then you are negating the atoning work of Christ at Calvary! You belong to the intimate and select group who have been given access to the Father's throne. It is free but not cheap. That is, it is free to you, but it cost Christ His life for you to have that privilege. Won't you take advantage of what is rightfully yours in Christ?

Satan's only tool in attacking us is to get us to neglect what is rightfully ours in Christ. He only knows how to rob and steal. But we are aware of our adversary, the devil, and we are not tricked by his devices. We are more than conquerors through Him that loved us! AMEN!

Conclusions: Get Ready
to Be Used!

△

Recently, I felt a burden to fast. Although my schedule was such that I needed my strength, I could not ignore the "still small voice" of the Holy Spirit directing me. I skipped the evening meal with my family. The next morning, I did not have breakfast and at lunch, I knew I was supposed to fast. Speaking to a ministers meeting in the morning, the Businessman's Fellowship in the afternoon and the Missions Department that evening, I was taxed physically; however, my spirit was buoyed by the knowledge that God was directing me. That evening again I knew I was to fast. Why was the Lord directing me to fast? I had no answer. I did not know of any purpose until the next morning.

The next morning while praying, I told the Lord, "Dear Heavenly Father, I am available for whatever You want. Although I don't know exactly what You want me to do, I know I am willing, able and ready to obey You."

As I arrived at my office, I found a couple from our church waiting to see me. "Pastor Cho," the mother, her face showing stress, said, "Last night our little girl lost most of her sight. We were at dinner As she picked up her spoon, she told us that she

176 ACOVENANT IN CHRIST JESUS

could not see it." Picking up a handkerchief to wipe away the tears
that were falling freely down her cheeks, she continued, "Then
she told us she could not see her socks and shoes. So we rushed
her to the hospital."

As I continued to listen to her story, I suddenly knew why I had
been fasting. "What did the doctors say?" I asked.

"The doctors told us that she had an inflamed optical nerve
which showed signs of decay. After closer examination, the doctors said that her central nervous system was also affected and she
would be paralyzed in her mid-section."

The mother then went on to describe their condition: "We are
really afraid that our daughter may be paralyzed, blinded and
may even die. We are really discouraged. Pastor Cho, what can
we do?"

I explained that I would pray for her and then visit her in the
hospital. I could give them assurance in faith because I knew that
the Holy Spirit had been preparing me for this battle with Satan
throughout my prayer and fasting.

The next morning, as I walked into the girl's room in the hospital, I was told that during the night her condition had improved.
My faith being built up during my fasting, I was able to pray with
great boldness, binding every evil force trying to destroy this
child of God. The doctors were amazed at the quick recovery the
girl experienced as a result of the prayer of faith. Now the girl is
whole by the grace and mercy of God.

Why do I share this story with you?

God is looking for men and women who will be His emergency
task force to combat the forces of the devil. The Holy Spirit wants
volunteers who will be at full alert whenever there is a crisis. I
have told the Holy Spirit that I wish to be on that task force of
spiritual volunteers.

We are at a crucial point in the history of the church. The
enemy knows that the hour is late and is poised to attack every
Christian family, church and organization. We have been assigned by God as the salt of the earth. Will we fulfill our responsibility—or will we ignore the signs of the times?

My purpose in sharing with you these few biblical principles and personal experiences is to motivate you to begin to pray. The hour is not too late to begin a life of prayer. If you desire revival, there has never been, nor are there now, any short cuts to revival. The only key to revival is prayer. However, it must begin in you and me. Allow the Holy Spirit to spark your life with the match of faith! Let the spark spread throughout your entire church, causing a fire that will eventually engulf your city, state and nation. Let it begin now! If not now, when? If not you, who? If not here, where?

Please pray with me: "Dear Holy Spirit, fill me now with Your power. Cause me to desire a life of prayer. Cause me to see the need and volunteer in Your prayer army. I pray this in the name of Jesus Christ, the Lord. AMEN!"

Study Guide

The questions and exercises in this study guide are designed for individual study which will in turn lead to group interaction. Thus, they may be used either as a guide for individual meditation or group discussion. During your first group meeting we suggest that you set aside a few minutes at the outset in which individual group members introduce themselves and share a little about their personal pilgrimage of faith.

If possible, it is a good idea to rotate leadership responsibility among the group members. However, if one individual is particularly gifted as a discussion leader, elect or appoint that person to guide the discussions each week. Remember, the leader's responsibility is simply to guide the discussion and stimulate interaction. He or she should never dominate the proceedings. Rather, the leader should encourage all members of the group to participate, expressing their individual views. He or she should seek to keep the discussion on track, but encourage lively discussion.

If one of the purposes of your group meeting is to create a caring community, it is a good idea to set aside some time for sharing individual concerns and prayer for one another. This can take the form of both silent and spoken petitions and praise.

1. What Prayer Accomplishes

1. Dr. Cho cites Moses, Joshua, David, and other Old Testament characters as men of prayer. Contrast their prayer lives with that of Jesus in the New Testament.

2. The author talks about the "power of prayer." Put that concept in your own words.

3. How does one's prayer life affect the rest of his life?

4. "The purpose of God is to break but not crush." What do you think the author means by this statement?

5. How does prayer help us in our ongoing battle with Satan?

6. Discuss the relationship between prayer and knowing the will of God.

2. Prayer and the Holy Spirit

1. How do we become aware of the Holy Spirit?

2. Is the Holy Spirit an "experience" or a "personality" to you (see p. 44)?

3. React to Dr. Cho's statement on page 45: "Just as the Holy Spirit caused Mary to conceive, so the Holy Spirit can impregnate us with the Living Word."

4. How can we "fellowship" with the Holy Spirit on a daily basis?

5. React to the statement on page 51: "Those who have not developed their spiritual sensitivity can only partake of the milk of God's Word."

3. Your Personal Response to Prayer

1. What do you think of Dr. Cho's idea of a "prayer-account balance"?

2. React to the author's statement on page 54: "We don't know how long we have to pray before God will answer our prayers."

3. "Some prayers require a great deal of repetition for there to be a response," says the author (p. 55). What kinds of prayer do you think Dr. Cho is talking about here?

4. Analyze Dr. Cho's formula on page 57: ". . . we can live our lives full of great peace. We have to give our problems to the Lord in prayer. We can therefore live healthy lives."

4. Prayer Is Petition

1. Note the prayer principles from "The Lord's Prayer" listed on page 62: praise, expectation, petition, confession, trust. Can you think of any other ingredients effective prayer should have?

2. On page 67 Dr. Cho says that "we must participate actively" in the answer to our needs by asking. What does he mean by this statement?

3. What does it mean to "ask in faith"?

4. How does God answer our petitions?

5. Dr. Cho says that "sociological and economic conditions dictate our faith level" (p. 71). Comment.

5. Prayer Is Devotion

1. The next level of prayer, says Dr. Cho, is "seeking." What does it mean to "seek" God?

2. What did the apostle Paul receive as a result of this kind of prayer?

3. What does "communion with God" mean to you?

4. "The lazy Christian is not willing to seek," says Dr. Cho on page 76. Describe the "lazy Christian" he mentions here.

6. Prayer Is Intercession

1. What are the qualities of an intercessor (p. 81)?

2. Why is intercession necessary?

3. What are the qualities of salt that are to be true of us as Christians?

4. Comment on the picture of Moses as an intercessor.

5. What door do we enter when we intercede in prayer?

7. Your Personal Devotional Life

1. What practice will "guarantee" our personal growth as Christians?

2. What two reasons does the author emphasize for praying on a daily basis?

3. Why are the morning hours usually best for Bible study?

4. What time of the day works best for you?

8. Your Family Devotions

1. Does your family have a regular devotional time together?

2. If not, based on Dr. Cho's rationale for family devotions, what can you do to establish a regular and effective devotional time?

3. If you have younger children, what method or book might you use to make the Bible more meaningful to your children?

4. What kind of prayer would be most meaningful to your family?

9. Prayer in the Church Service

1. Is prayer as prominent in the services of your church as it seems to be in Dr. Cho's?

2. In the author's opinion, the power of prayer seems to be multiplied in direct proportion to the number praying. What are the implications of that truth?

10. Prayer at the Cell Meetings

1. Why is the "cell system" so effective in large churches? Read Romans 16:5; Acts 2:46–47, 5:42, 6:4, 20:20.

2. Why do large churches tend to be more impersonal than small churches?

3. If the small group concept is not already in use in your church, what do you think you could do to implement it?

11. Prayer at Prayer Mountain

1. How could the "prayer mountain" concept be adapted to your church?

2. In your experience, is there a place where you feel closer to God than any other?

3. Do you think the sheer volume of prayer at Prayer Mountain is the key to the success of Dr. Cho's ministry?

12. All-Night Prayer Meetings

1. Do you know of any American churches that make it a practice to have all-night prayer vigils?

2. What other biblical examples of all-night prayer can you find in the Scriptures?

3. Where does time pass most swiftly and pleasantly for you?

4. Is there any way you can make that time or place a prayer altar as well?

13. Fasting and Prayer

1. Do you agree with Dr. Cho that the path to more power in prayer includes fasting?

2. Dr. Cho cites Jesus and Paul as examples of "fasting and prayer" (see Acts 13 and 14). Can you think of other New Testament examples? Old Testament?

3. "Fasting and prayer brings clarity of mind," says Dr. Cho. Is there a physical as well as a spiritual reason for this?

4. "The stronger the desire, the more effective the prayer," says Dr. Cho on page 116. Is this true in other realms as well? Discuss.

5. Note the connection between healing and prayer. What about the link between a forgiving spirit and prayer?

6. What is the connection between pride and an unforgiving spirit?

7. What physical health benefits are there in fasting?

14. Waiting on the Lord

1. Compare the law of specificity in prayer to the need for focus in meditation.

2. What are some specific spiritual subject areas upon which you can meditate?

3. What Bible character would you choose as your model in meditation?

4. Dr. Cho says that God's work demands ". . . strength that goes beyond youth and natural ability" (p. 128). Can you think of a specific person in your acquaintance who personifies that truth? How about a Bible character?

15. Developing Persistence in Prayer

1. Dr. Cho equates persistence in prayer with the length of time spent in earnest petition. How long do you normally spend in daily prayer?

2. Do you make it a practice to pray for specific needs?

3. Do you devote equal time to praise and petition?

4. In our world of "instant everything," have we Americans lost depth in our prayer lives?

5. When does petition in prayer become "vain"?

16. Praying in the Holy Spirit

1. What does it mean to pray "in the Spirit"?

2. What does it mean to you to know the Holy Spirit makes intercession for you (Rom. 8:26)?

3. Is praying in the Spirit limited to the use of a "prayer language"?

4. God is looking for our willingness in order to work His will. How do we get our wills in line with His?

17. The Prayer of Faith

1. "Faith in prayer (is not) optional," says Dr. Cho. "We must have faith . . . for our prayer to be heard" (p. 147). Discuss this spiritual precept.

2. What are the three basic steps in the prayer of faith?

3. What are some of your "visions and dreams"? Name some people with whom you have shared these dreams.

4. What obstacles get in the way of your prayer of faith?

18. Listening to God's Voice

1. "Prayer is a dialogue, not a monologue," says Dr. Cho on page 153. Comment.

2. What does it mean to have "an ear to hear"?

3. How do we develop the "hearing ear"?

4. "By learning to listen to God, we will not be caught unaware," says Dr. Cho on page 158. Discuss the implications of this statement.

19. The Importance of Group Prayer

1. In group prayer, says Dr. Cho, "the power of our faith is increased geometrically" (p. 161). Discuss.

2. Discuss the geometric progression of faith described on page 163.

3. What is the only thing that can hinder prayer?

20. Powerful Prayer

1. What is a covenant?

2. Who are the parties in the covenant described in this chapter?

3. What was Christ's part in the divine covenant?

4. What were God's promises to Christ?

5. We approach the Father in the name Christ. What does that mean?

6. Through prayer we are more than conquerors. What does this mean?

Send prayer requests to

Paul Cho Ministries
33743 Ninth Avenue South
Federal Way, WA 98003